To my team
My partner in life and business Melinda
My sons Tom and Jack
My daughters Scout and Indigo

# GROW:3
## TEAM

**Have you got what it takes
to build a great team?**

Antony Whitaker

**"**

"You can dream, create, design and build the most wonderful place in the world but it takes **people** to make the dream a reality."

**Walt Disney**

# About the author

Antony Whitaker is a seminar presenter, coach, motivational business educator and author, specialising in small businesses with a focus on the hairdressing industry.

GROW: 3 Team is Antony's third book following the success of GROW: 1 Super Stylist and GROW: 2 Management

'GROW: 3 Team' is about what it takes to build and be part of a great team.

Antony's experiences building his own teams in the hairdressing sector and coaching many business owners the world over has given him a unique insight into the skills required to succeed at building a team in any small business.

In keeping with the tone of the first two books 'GROW: 3 'Team' is written in the same no-nonsense direct style, offering practical advice which is based on real experience.

Antony Whitaker is acknowledged globally as one of the hairdressing industry's most passionate educators. He travels widely, presenting powerful motivational seminars on management, money, marketing, team building, retailing and customer service.

Antony's talents have taken him to over forty countries presenting to in excess of 250,000 people. His past accolades include winning the Grand Trophy of the Professional Press Association and twice winner of Australian Hairdresser of the Year; he has won awards for marketing, salon design, photography, salon team and education.

Originally from New Zealand, Antony has spent much of his life in both Australia and London and currently lives in the United Kingdom with his wife Melinda and their two daughters.

For more information, seminar details and subscription to a complimentary newsletter packed with advice and helpful tips, visit: www.growmysalonbusiness.com

# Acknowledgements

I have been in the hair and beauty industry for in excess of 30 years and I have been fortunate to work with some amazing people and privileged to work on some great teams, including the team I am with now.

If we live and work in isolation of others, then we limit our potential. All through our lives we are forming bonds, building relationships and creating communities or 'teams' to belong to, to be part of.

We are defined from our early beginnings and throughout our lives by those relationships…with our family, our church, our football clubs, our schools, our social partnerships and our professional peer groups. Each of us becomes who we are, by who we surround ourselves with. We are products of our varied environments, products of our relationships and products of the teams we join.

Like you, all through my life I have had friends and professional relationships that have formed me into the person I am.

So a heartfelt 'Thank You!' To my children, Tom, Jack, Scout and Indigo, my wife Melinda, my late mum and dad, my brothers and sisters and all my extended family and of course my friends and colleagues who have influenced me along the path of my journey.

In getting this book into your hands, I am as always hugely indebted to Rachel Gould for her guidance and journalistic skills in editing and refining this book.

Thanks also to Karen Wilks for her creativity with the graphic design of this book and in understanding my vision and the market to which I appeal. Her skill and patience as a graphic designer has helped to present my thoughts and words in a way that compliments perfectly my subject and content in a vibrant and creative manner.

Each of us is the product of our life experiences; the books we read and the people we listen to and learn from have an influence on us. They shape the people that we are and the people we become. Over the years I have read a lot of business books and attended a lot of seminars and many people have influenced me.

As an author and presenter I would like to acknowledge the following people, some of whom I have met and worked with. There are many more that have influenced my work through reading their material, attending their seminars or spending time in their company. All of the following people have at some level inspired me in business and unknowingly contributed to the contents of this book. Where I am able, I acknowledge individuals as the source if I directly quote their material.

Many of them share an ethos so it is sometimes difficult to accurately quote an original source, however all of them have books worth reading or seminars worth attending in your quest to develop as an individual and a business.

Anthony Robbins, Michael Gerber, Robert Kiyosaki, Seth Godin, Drayton Bird, John Maxwell, Frank Kern, Tom Hopkins, Brian Tracy, Tom Peters, Wayne Dyer, Earl Nightingale, Zig Ziglar, W Mitchell, Jim Rohn, Ken Blanchard, Sam Parker, Jonathan Jay, W Edwards Demming, Robert Cialdini, Dr Stefanie Burns, Malcolm Gladwell, Steve Jobs, Conrad Levinson, Robert Greene, Peter Drucker, Marcus Buckingham, Daniel Pink, Dale Carnegie, Stephen Covey, Buckminster Fuller, Michael Shergold, Hugh Williams, Brad Sugars, Neil Ducoff, Simon Lotinga, Wynne Claybaugh, Blair Singer, Dr Joanna Martin, Spencer Johnson, Nigel Risner, Geoffrey Gitomer, Dan Kennedy, Alan Pease, Al Ries, Jack Trout, Sam Parker, Daniel Goleman, Dr Harry Alder, Richard Templar, John Dijulius, Robert Greene, Kevin Roberts, Peter Fisk, Scott Stratten...

Finally thank you to everyone who bought my first two books and thank you to the many people all over the world that subscribe to my newsletter, attend my seminars and keep in touch via Facebook. We have now established quite a growing community (dare we call it a team?) and it's a great privilege to be involved in your life even in a virtual capacity.

# Thank You!

# Table of Contents

# Introduction
## Who are you?

No matter where in life you look, whether it's music, sport, politics or business, you will see that great accomplishments are not achieved by one individual alone but by a team of people all working together with a common goal. If you look behind every winner you will see in the background a great support team that might include great coaches, managers, mentors and role models, families, partners, friends and colleagues.

**Neil Armstrong** was the first man on the moon but there was a TEAM of thousands that made that happen.

**Sir Edmund Hillary** was the first to scale Mount Everest but there was a TEAM behind him.

**Usain Bolt** may be the fastest man in history but there is a TEAM behind him.

**Steve Jobs** may have been the iconic figurehead of Apple but there was a TEAM behind him.

**Vidal Sassoon** was the legendary figure behind the brand, but there was a TEAM behind him.

From Toni & Guy, Trevor Sorbie, Jacque Dessange ...you name it, any successful brand in our industry or any other industry, will have dozens of people cheering them on. Every successful endeavour is the result of many people working together, sharing in the vision,

So, who are you? Who do I imagine you to be? Who is my book written for? What do I assume you want to take away from reading this?

# In short…what's it all about?

What is important to me is that this book isn't just theory, it's definitely NOT a text book. This is the real stuff and like my previous books, GROW: 3 Team, will connect with you in a meaningful way because the content has relevance to your life, today!

I often ask my seminar audience "…what are the top three challenges you face in your business…" the answers are pretty much the same everywhere I go.

In descending order of priority the third biggest challenge is 'the staff', the second biggest challenge is…'the staff' and the number one biggest challenge is…you guessed it, 'the staff'! From Mumbai to London, from Shanghai to New York, the biggest challenges we face are our people. Finding them, training them, motivating them, keeping them, inspiring them.

Our team is our business and our success revolves around how well we handle those challenges, this book is about addressing those challenges. There is no magic wand, no set of instructions that will solve all your problems and it's a job that is never finished. To be frank it's about hard work but if you get it right, the rewards are enormous.

This book is a collection of powerful ideas, distilled from my personal learning experience and harvested from those that I have had the fortune to meet and learn from along the way. Building your team is a never ending job. The ideas expressed in this book are not right or wrong, they're just ideas that worked for me and I know most of them will work for you. You decide what is right for your business, your team, your vision and your culture.

# So, who are you? What are your dreams and ambitions? What are your challenges and frustrations?

I assume that you are probably in the hair and beauty business, perhaps you are new to the industry or maybe you are a stylist, colourist or beauty therapist. In all probability you are an owner or manager of others ...regardless, I am happy to say that, "I have walked a mile in those shoes". We have common ground. I have experienced the challenges and frustrations of the stylist and later became an owner/manager. In my journey I too have built teams to take me (and them) where they wanted to go. I have had the fun and laughter, the tears and frustration, the disappointments and euphoria.

{ I think I understand you, and I think you'll understand me }

In other words; "I think I understand you, and I think you'll understand me."

## How to use this book...

You can use this book as you wish, however, if it is going to be more than an interesting collection of ideas and instead be a tool to improve your skills and develop a dream team, then the following points may be of some help.

- Arm yourself with a highlighter pen and don't be afraid to use it. When you read something that touches a nerve with you highlight it! The reason I do that is so that you can skim through the text at a later stage and the key points jump out at you
- Don't be defensive justifying why something can't or won't work for you in your salon, your country etc. Have an open mind, try the ideas out, see what works, reject what doesn't or adapt it to your salon and your culture so that it does work but make sure you give it a go.
- Flag important pages with Post-it notes.
- Set a list of goals of things that you are going to do!
- Do them! Pick your top 3 objectives and make a start.

I have structured this book in a series of chapters, 6 in total. You can read it from cover to cover if you choose, or can just dip in and out of the chapters or subject headings that seem the most relevant to you.

Chapter 1, 'Teams need leaders', focuses on the importance of 'leadership and vision' and why as the leader you need to continually build on your leadership skills and develop an inspiring vision for others to follow.

Chapter 2 is titled 'Who is on your team?' and as the heading says it's about the people that make up a team and identifies why you need to build and be part of a team to reach your goals.

Chapter 3 is titled 'Creating your team culture' and is about how you get the team that you plan for. Every team has a culture. Your business, clients and the individuals on the team can benefit from a team culture that is supportive or in many cases one that has unfortunately developed over time and constantly changes based on the whims of the people on the team.

> If you keep doing the right things, the right things will happen

Chapter 4 titled 'Training: building a culture of excellence' is a summary of the training systems that need to be in place to ensure team standards and continuity.

Chapter 5, 'Communication' focuses on the importance of developing effective communication strategies within the team.

Chapter 6, titled 'Maintaining your team' is about developing long term strategies to keep your team evolving and dealing with change.

One thing I have learned is that there is no magic wand or short cuts and I certainly don't profess to have all the answers but as the late Vidal Sassoon once said "If you keep doing the right things, the right things will happen". There are some things in life that you just have to believe and trust and in my opinion that statement is certainly one of those things.

So take what you want from this book, take what feels right for you and your team, for your culture your country and for the dreams that you have for your life and if just one of these ideas contributes to your growth and team success then I have achieved my goal with this book.

↑ Lesson: "if nothing changes ...nothing changes".

# "No man is an Island"

I assume that applies to woman as well. That quote is from John Donne (1572-1631) a poet not a hairdresser or beauty therapist, but the sentiment is spot on, *"No man [or woman] is an island"*

GROW: 3 TEAM is about recognising that your success as an individual and the success of the business has a lot to do with building and belonging to a great team because *"No man is an island"*. So, in other words…you can't do it alone.

## It started with an idea.

That is where it all started isn't it? You had this idea. It wasn't a goal or a vision, it was merely an idea.

## It was the idea that you could do it better!

The idea that there was a better way. The idea of how it could be done, how it should be done, and how you will do it. It was your idea and it grew into your dream, your goal, your vision for how you wanted your salon, your business, your team to be. The problem is that ideas are two a penny; everyone has a good idea at some point. For your idea, or in fact any idea, to be realised it needs to be carefully nurtured and defined by you, the leader. You are the 'guardian of the idea' but you can't do it alone.

If you are the owner or manager, then that is one of your roles… to be the guardian of the idea. In order for you and your business to grow you need to attract others that believe in your idea, people that share the same dream and are prepared to follow you 'the leader'. That's what a team is, 'people connected to each other by a leader and a shared belief in an idea.

# Where do you start?

Different people have different expectations from a job. A successful team will share common goals, a common purpose, a common vision and values. If you start off with a group of people who are already aligned in their vision, values and purpose, then you have a strong foundation to build on.

Alternatively if you employ people without understanding what is important to them in life and people that don't understand the goals and values of the business, you risk a situation where the team is fragmented before you start. From the outset your business is rife with differences of opinion and conflicting agendas.

Understanding this is to understand the very essence of what makes a team work.

# Creating the winning team

Any relationship can only survive and flourish if it is based on the idea of win:win. In other words it has to be beneficial for all parties. The success and longevity of the business and the team within it, is entwined with the individuals' success. The only way the business or the team wins is if the individual wins and vice versa

On the assumption that your business is not some sort of workers co-operative but is an employee-employer model and an independently owned business, then not everyone on the team will be equal, someone has to be the boss. It is also inevitable that there will be degrees of hierarchy and differing levels of responsibility but we are all part of the team and the whole team needs to win.

I believe that more often than not we all want the team to work so that we all win but often people on the team have different ideas of what winning looks like and only view it from their perspective.

The key to get a **win:win** is to build a team that:
• shares the same values
• shares the same vision
• honours an agreed code of conduct
• has strong visionary leadership

If everyone has a different vision of success, different values, different priorities and different rules to play by then that is not a team and it can't result in a win:win. The very nature of a team is getting everyone's vision, values and conduct aligned. Businesses that are aligned get where they want faster and so do the individuals that work in them. To make that happen a team needs leadership!

## As the leader, your job is to align the people on your team and to unite them in a common goal.

So where do we start? We start at the beginning and that means re-evaluating the very fundamentals of your business and looking at the core values, culture and vision of the business.

↑ Lesson: For the team relationship to survive and flourish it needs to be based on the principle of win:win, it has to be beneficial for all concerned.

# 1

## YOUR TEAM NEEDS A VISIONARY LEADER

# First, you need to lead and they will follow...

A team requires the leader's commitment, their leader's belief in the idea and their leader's intention to turn that idea into reality. Without belief, commitment and intention from the leader, the team is going nowhere. These elements shape leadership and attract and bond a tight knit team.

{ without leaders, there are no followers... }

As Seth Godin say's in his excellent book 'Tribes',"without leaders, there are no followers. You're a leader. We need you"

Being the leader doesn't mean that you have to have all the answers, no one does but, it does mean that you have courage. You need to have the courage to begin, to risk, to challenge the status quo, to 'have a go' and if [or when] you fail, to have the courage to get up and do it all again and again and again.

Everyone on the team has something to contribute. There are no mistakes, there are no coincidences; everyone is there for a reason, even the 'rat-bags' [and there will be some] are there to teach you something. The question is 'what is it?' Take the time to see the lesson that you are meant to gain from their presence on your team?

## Will you make mistakes?

Most definitely, everyday in all probability but as the saying goes "if you're not making mistakes, you're not making anything".

↑ Lesson: It starts with you... 'the leader'.

If you're not making mistakes, you're not making anything

# Leadership and vision go hand in hand

People are looking for leadership, most people don't have the courage to have big dreams but they will follow others who have the vision and leadership skills to turn it into reality.

I once heard it said that, "A business is a reflection of its leader". If, you are like me, you didn't really want to be told that at the time. I suppose it is because it showed that my situation highlighted all of my weaknesses. It reinforced that everything that goes on in your business is either a reflection of your ability or inability. In essence you get the staff and the business you deserve.

So have a look at your business, try to be objective and recognise that the weaknesses in the business are most likely a reflection of your own weaknesses. If you can take ownership of that [and some people never will, as they are determined to blame someone else for their problems and shortcomings] then the real question becomes...

{ A business is a reflection of its leader }

## "What can you and what will you do about it?"

In my previous book titled 'GROW 2: Management' there is a section about developing your business vision but the purpose of this book is to talk about vision and leadership in the context of team building, so from here on the emphasis is less on the owner as leader but the issues that surround leadership and the importance of having a vision in the context of your team.

↑ Lesson: "Every team needs a leader. You're it, so lead"

"Your greatest responsibility is to be a leader, **a visionary.** Leadership is what attracts and keeps people."

# If your vision doesn't inspire you, it's not going to inspire anyone else either.

"But I just want to cut hair and have fun…
I don't want to have all this vision stuff."

Sorry! I thought you wanted to own a vibrant, profitable, growing business of your own; a business that gave you a great lifestyle and fulfilled your creative ambitions. Well, if that's the case, turning it into a reality involves a lot more than just cutting hair and having fun. If you're like most salon owners you had a vision, and the vision was 'to have your own salon' and you had a plan to turn it into reality. Congratulations you did it! The problem is that often, that is where the vision and the plan ended. Now the only vision you have is to survive and the only plan you have is to work yourself to the bone doing it. That's a lousy vision and a lousy plan.

{ For a vision to be understood everyone must be part of it }

## What does all this have to do with team work?

A vision is what attracts and keeps people on your team. For a vision to be understood everyone must be part of it, contribute to it and believe in it. A vision unites a team to a common purpose by sharing common rules, performance goals, standards and behaviours. So having a 'vision' has a lot to do with team work.

Think of a football team or any great athlete, when they go out onto the field they all have a very clear vision of what their desired outcome is for the game, they want to win! They have a game plan and they all understand their role and responsibilities. They actively visualise winning the game, the tournament, the league, the medal. They have a vision and a very clear focus of what needs to be done to achieve it.

*Sharing a common vision is what unites a team*

## What is your vision for your business?

If you're serious about building a team you better have a vision for the business and the team, or your team building days are over and your business is going nowhere.

↑ **Lesson: A vision is what attracts and keeps people on your team. For a vision to be understood everyone must be part of it, contribute to it and believe in it.**

"

"The essence of a **team** is a common **commitment**. Without it groups perform as individuals; with it, they become a powerful unit of collective performance. This kind of commitment requires a purpose in which team members can believe. Your role is to develop that purpose, that **vision!**"

# It is essential that everyone on the team understand the vision for the business

What is the vision for the business? What is it that you are trying to achieve? What will it feel like? How will it operate? What will the team aspire to represent and stand for?

The problems often start with the fact that the individuals on the team want different things, they have different goals and aspirations as to how they think the business should operate so they are effectively pulling in different directions and as a result are pulling the team apart. As a team you need to have a collective vision that everyone on the team shares and that everyone understands and 'buys into.'

The problem is that you can't 'share a vision' if you don't have one. The role of the leader is to create and define the vision for the business and to build a team of people who share in that vision and share in the determination to turn it into a reality. Without a 'shared vision' the individuals on the team will do what is easiest for them, which may or may not be what is best for the team and the business. The vision is the starting point for everything the 'team' achieves and it underpins everything that comes afterwards. The vision is the goal, a direction, a purpose.

{ The vision is the goal, a direction, a purpose }

Every great team shares a common vision and out of the vision comes a plan. If it is a strong and compelling vision it works like a magnet pulling everyone on the team towards it.

What is your vision, your goal for your salon?
Is your vision in alignment with the rest of the team and the business goals?

Only you know the answer to that but part of the salon's success and your success is in being on a team where you share the same vision/goals, values, beliefs…

What vision do you have as a team for the business?
• What are the goals, both short and long term?
• Does everyone know what they are?
• Does everyone agree with them?
• How will you measure your success?

↑ Lesson: A shared vision is a common goal, a shared vision is having everyone on the team with the same focus and everyone moving in the same direction united in their commitment to achieve an agreed outcome. If you don't want the same things as the business and the rest of the team, what are you doing there? And most importantly what are you going to do about it?

# No single person can make the team be a team...

No single person can make the team be a team; everybody has a responsibility in building and maintaining the team dynamic.

The leader, manager or coach can put in place the vision, the structure and the systems  but everyone has a role and a responsibility in making the team, 'a team.' Everyone on the team has a degree of ownership and accountability in the success or failure of the team. We all want to be part of a team of people that have a real bond, a team that really support and care about each other, not a 'Team of Champions' but a 'Championship Team.'

A 'Championship Team' is a team where everyone recognises that they are part of something bigger than just themselves. A 'Championship Team' is a team where everyone has an essential contribution to make, regardless of whether they are a first day assistant or a creative director, everyone has a very important role to play in developing, contributing to, and participating in the team.

> { In a 'Championship Team' the total is far greater than the sum of its parts }

That is what is meant by the phrase "the synergy of teams", where 1 + 1 + 1 doesn't equal 3, it equals 5 or 10 or ...the total is far greater than the sum of its parts.

That team synergy occurs when a group of individuals collectively perform to a level far beyond their capability as individuals whether in sport, in music, in families, in politics or in your business. In a 'Championship Team' the total is far greater than the sum of its parts.

↑ Lesson: Synergy is the elusive magic that turns the ordinary into the extraordinary. Synergy is a collective consciousness, a mutual understanding where the individuals think and act as if they were one.

# 1 + 1 + 1

# Not a
'Team of Champions'
## but a
'Championship Team'

# Turning the vision into a reality...

Coming up with a vision is the first step but how can we help turn the vision into a reality?

- How can you better clarify and define the team vision?
- How can you better communicate the vision to yourself and the rest of your team?
- How can you better involve the rest of the team so that they all believe in the vision?
- How can you create more leverage to help your team mates achieve their goals?

The more you get the 'buy-in' of those on your team the more likely they will be committed to making the vision a reality. So what are some ways we can increase the likelihood that the individuals on your team will take ownership of the vision and be as committed as you to realising it?

{ It's your vision so express it in a way that works for you. }

**1. Brainstorm it with the team so that they take more ownership.**
Instead of just giving the team the end result of the 'owners vision' and expecting them to embrace it, sit down together as a team and facilitate a brainstorming session on creating an appropriate vision. Integrate as many of their ideas as possible so that you really do arrive at a team vision.

**2. Write it down and continually refine it.**
As I said, it needn't be Shakespeare, make a start and commit to refining it over time. There is no right or wrong, it's your vision so express it in a way that works for you.

**3. Identify and reaffirm the reasons why.**
A goal is more likely to become reality if you have strong reasons why it's attainment is important to you. If you can identify and focus on why you are doing it...'The what's in it for me' you will be more likely to stick with it during difficult times.

**4. Mind map and delegate key roles to teams or individuals.**
No one individual can do it all themselves, a successful business has many components to it, so the more you are able to integrate the team into the roles, goals and responsibilities the more evenly the load is spread and the more the team feel a real ownership and control over their destiny.

### 5. Review the company vision annually.

At the beginning of each year, take the time to sit down as a team and review the company vision. Some of the goals from the previous year may be carried over, others may have been achieved and now need replacing. It is an important process to redefine and future-proof the goals and the vision.

### 6. Teach them how to achieve it.

Don't assume that just because you have collectively come up with a vision that everyone knows how to achieve it. Having the goal is the first step, now you need to break it down into bite size action steps, so that it becomes reality

### 7. Read it every day and affirm your intentions.

It is all too easy to develop a series of noble goals but then life takes over and all too quickly your vision statement starts gathering dust on a book shelf. That is where the value of having written it down is evident. Whether you frame it and put it on the staff room wall or turn it into a screen saver or have it as page one in your diary, it is essential that you read it every day to re-affirm your intentions and keep on track.

### 8. Capture it visually on a picture board, chunk it down.

Consider developing a picture or mood board that captures the components of your vision statement. Bearing in mind that hairdressers are visually orientated people, having a picture board that encompasses your values and vision can be a very effective way of either stating or reinforcing the company or individual vision.

### 9. Discuss with the team their interpretation of words and pictures.

To keep the vision alive and integrated into the teams' daily actions it is important that you take the time to discuss their interpretation and understanding of the words, pictures and desired outcomes that are expressed in the vision statement.

↑ Lesson: The more you get the 'buy-in' of everyone on the team the more likely they will be committed to making the vision a reality. Everyone on the team needs to develop ways to communicate and live the vision to ensure that everyone is equally committed to the realisation of it.

How can I turn my vision into reality?

# Checklist Chapter 1:
# Your team needs a visionary leader

- A business is a reflection of its leaders. First you need to lead and they will follow.

- As the manager your greatest responsibility is to be a 'leader.' If you don't lead, who will?

- Leadership and vision go hand-in-hand. You need to be very clear about the ways in which you will build a successful business.

- Everyone on the team has something to contribute; everyone on the team is there for a reason.

- A vision is what attracts and keeps people on your team. For a vision to be understood  everyone must be part of it, contribute to it and believe in it.

- Everyone on the team needs to understand and share the same vision and values

- What are some tangible things to do that will create a compelling vision for others to follow?

- Develop a mood board that visually captures your vision.

- Involve your team in developing your vision.

- Develop an inspiring emotive written vision statement and display it in the staffroom.

- Break the vision down into smaller pieces.

# 2

## WHO IS ON YOUR TEAM?

# We all need to belong...

As human beings we belong in packs, we always have and it is at a very primal level that we have this intense need to belong and be part of something bigger. We are drawn together and attracted to like minded people and led by the strongest, those with the ideas and the beliefs to carry it off. Being part of a great team is not just a case of turning up or being along for the ride and getting processed, nor is it about ticking off a list of theoretical and rational key steps that you read about in a book on team building. No, that won't even nearly achieve what you want to achieve.

Sure there is plenty of rational thinking and theory behind what it takes to build and be part of a great team but remember we are dealing with people and people are emotional beings. Long after they have forgotten the theory of what a person said, they will remember the emotion of how they felt.

Any great team, whether it's in a business, music, sport, politics, family or a couple in a relationship is full of emotion, passion and energy. Building and being part of a great team of people that work together is a never ending, emotionally driven living process.

But, most of all, being part of a team gives you the chance to grow and achieve beyond your capability as an individual.

## The only question is;
## 'Are you up for the challenge?'

↑ Lesson: Being part of a team is not something you can just pay lip service to. When you become part of a team, that is exactly what you are...part of a team and with every part comes risk and reward, highs and lows, opportunities and disappointments, rights and responsibilities, obligations and options.

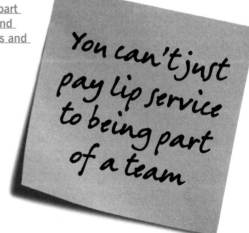

You can't just pay lip service to being part of a team

# What is a team, and why do you need to be part of it?

*"A team is a small number of people with complimentary skills who are committed to a common purpose, set of performance goals and approach for which they hold themselves mutually accountable."*

The key words in that statement are 'complimentary skills, committed, common purpose and mutually accountable'.

Remember what you are building is a 'Championship Team not a team of Champions'. In other words…

## not everyone scores the goals.

In business teams, as in a sporting teams, it is important to recognise that for the team to function at its best there needs to be a range of roles and functions. Inevitably some of those roles have more 'glory or prestige' attached to them, that doesn't make those roles more important as every role has an important function to perform and without all those functions being done the team can't operate effectively.

For example the superstar stylist cant operate at their peak without the superstar assistants who are doing the laundry, folding the towels, making the coffee, shampooing and so on or the equally fabulous receptionist who confirms all the bookings and manages the appointment book and co-ordinates the staff schedules and manages the stock levels....Every role is equally important, as every role is dependent on common best practise. You don't want a team of superstars all vying for a chance to be the 'top dog', you want a team of people all with clearly defined roles and functions to fulfil, so the client is the winner!

{ Every role has an important function to perform. }

Collectively they are all committed to a common vision which everyone on the team understands and buys into, they are all in it together and the collective result has a meaning. Everyone on the team has a role to play in delivering that result, from the new assistant who might be on their first day, to the manager or creative director who may be a 40 year plus veteran, it's a real team effort …and you need to be part of that team.

↑ Lesson: Don't get confused about what you're trying to build, a Championship Team will always outperform a team of Champions. The very nature of teams is that everyone has a role to fulfil in bringing about the end goal…happy clients and a vibrant team culture.

"Your future success, now more than ever, is determined by your ability to **nurture**, **evolve**, train and maintain a team. You grow people into a team that represents your brand."

# You just read your job description...

Or at least part of it.

I'm assuming you either own a business, manage a business, aspire to owning a business or at least plan on understanding how some businesses thrive where others fail. It's the magic ingredient 'team work' and it's not just a word it's a way of collectively being.

## Your role amongst other things is to: nurture, build, evolve, train and maintain a team.

You 'grow people' into a team that represents your brand. The day you open a business a number of forces conspire to determine the success or otherwise of the business. Typically because we are in an image business, the things we pay most attention to at the beginning are the visuals, the aesthetics of the salon décor the graphics, the logo, the interior design the appearance of the staff, the presentation of everything.

{ The managers role is to turn the vision into a reality }

Very quickly the reality sets in that what really sets a business apart is the people that work in it. Not just the quality of the individuals from a technical and creative perspective, but the mix of talents, the attitudes, the communication, how they have fun, how they resolve conflict, the respect, the trust, the leadership and how they connect as a team. Unfortunately none of that just happens because you want it to. If that's what you want to happen on your team and I believe it is, then as the manager that is your job.

↑ Lesson: The managers role is to turn the vision into a reality, and what's more, if you or someone else in the business is not consciously doing that, then don't kid yourself...it's not happening, and you're paying an enormous price as a result.

# Roles, goals and responsibilities...

In my earlier book 'GROW 2 Management' we addressed 'roles, goals and responsibilities' in the context of the four 'business functions' meaning finance, marketing, HR and operations. Now in the context of your team we need to look at the 'roles, goals and responsibilities' operationally as a 'Salon Team'.

## For your team to function smoothly there needs to be very clearly defined roles, goals and responsibilities.

Those different roles all have different names. In the hair and beauty industry those roles have titles like, stylist, receptionist, assistant, etc. Accompanying each role or position there needs to be a job description that clearly defines the goals and responsibilities of that position. Different size businesses determine what roles, goals and responsibilities you have on the team but you can't build a team until you and everyone else on the team is clear about them, from doing the laundry to being the salon 'Training Manager'.

The best way to do this exercise is with an 'Organisation Chart.'

## Take a blank piece of paper.

Now, as you are probably the manager put your name in a box titled 'owner' at the centre top of the page and leave plenty of room underneath to develop 'a tree' that reflects the 'ideal' organisation chart for your salon.

Define the roles goals and responsibilities of everyone on the team

Step 1: On the assumption that you want to develop a chart that represents your salon at its maximum capacity you first need to decide what that is. For example, in the chart below based on the physical size and number of chairs in the salon you might decide that the maximum number of team members you can have including yourself is 15.

Step 2: What is the business model that you are going to have? For example:
• Will you have a manager or assistant manager, or is that you?
• Will you have a receptionist?
• Will you have a salon co-ordinator?
• Will you have assistants?
• Will you have separate stylists and colourists?
• Will you have different levels of stylists and colourists?
• Is there a training role(s)?
• What are the names/titles that you will give to these roles?
• What other roles might you have, i.e. cleaner, cloakroom, beauty department, manicurists, therapists, retail educator etc

Step 3: Once you have decided the business model, the number of positions, the different roles and the respective titles that you will work with, then you are able to develop a chart and fill in the boxes with the relevant 'positions' to show the ideal scenario.

{ Be aware that the names you give have a real effect }

Step 4: Lastly fill in corresponding 'names' of the people that hold that position, or if there is no one in a particular position leave it blank as an unfilled position.

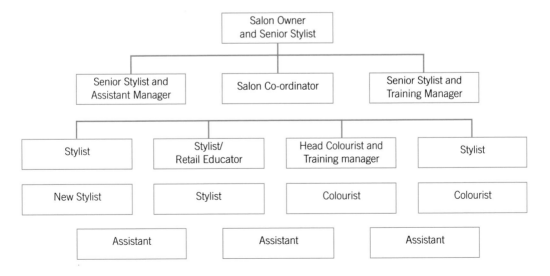

GROW / 33

One final thought before we move on. This is just a suggested model not a definitive structure or title for any position. Only you can decide whether you will have different levels of stylists/colourists, training roles, assistants, receptionists etc. But, be aware that the names you give a position have a real affect on establishing an identity and level of responsibility that the position holds.

**For example:**
    Junior stylist or New Stylist
    Receptionists or Salon Co-ordinator or Front of House
    Cleaner or Housekeeper
    Creative Director or Training Manager

So, who is on your team? What are you going to call the various positions? What functions do they fill and what are you missing?

**You now have a personnel map of how your salon will look.**

As a salon manager, if you don't already have them you need to develop job descriptions, 'policy and procedure' manuals and an organisation chart that clearly defines the roles, goals and responsibilities of everyone on your team. Unfortunately many salons still don't have an organised and defined structure and as a result they typically aren't able to grow past a certain point. Without clearly defined roles, goals and responsibilities understood by everyone the business cannot function smoothly in a consistent and predictable manner.

Many young stylists look at this sort of thing as being too corporate and structured as they see the salon as a purely 'creative enterprise' but they are missing the point. It is! The systems and structures are not designed to inhibit and restrict their creativity but designed to allow them to concentrate on being creative because the systems and structures liberate their time to focus on the client with confidence, knowing that everything else will run smoothly in a predicable and consistent manner.

{ Everyone has a unique set of skills that they bring to the team }

↑ Lesson: Most people want to do a good job, often they just don't know what it is they are meant to be doing. Every team needs structure, systems and clearly defined roles, goals and responsibilities for every position.

# Everyone matters!

Everyone has a unique set of skills that they bring to the team. It doesn't matter if it is their first day on the team or if they have been there for 40 years they all matter. Their industry experience, their life experiences, their perspectives, their understanding and view of people and the world we live in is absolutely 100% unique to them and them alone. Everything they have done in life contributes to who they are at this point in time: from the family they were born into, how they were raised, the religions they have been exposed to, their country and culture, their education, the jobs they've had, the places they've been, the sports they've played, the people they've met, the conversations they've had, the friends they've made and the relationships they've had ...everything makes a difference. Everything conspires to make us the unique individuals we are today.

No one has done exactly what they have done, no one thinks exactly like them, no one has had all the same sequences of events and life experiences that they have had. All those experiences contribute to make them the person that they are, the person on your team. Don't underestimate how valuable a resource that is to you and to the rest of the team. No one has all the answers. A smart leader knows that, and they also understand the power of drawing on the experiences of everyone in the team.

In a seminar environment I will often go round the room and ask a random selection of 20 individuals two questions. First, how long have you been in the industry? Second, how many salons have you worked in?

Obviously from seminar to seminar the answers vary but there is one thing that is fairly consistent. When I add up the combined total number of salons and the combined total years in the industry, typically the answer arrives at in excess of 70 salons and in excess of 250 years. Imagine if those 20 people were all on your team, what a wealth of experience that is to draw on. Seventy plus salons and 250 plus years and that is just the salon experience. What about all the other experiences they have had, from previous jobs, perhaps working in other businesses to playing in various team sports and belonging to different groups and clubs. There is a huge, often untapped resource that resides in the hearts and minds of your team, if you can draw on it everyone in the team wins.

↑ Lesson: No one has all the answers! Everyone on the team has a unique and valuable contribution to make in how to build and maintain a team. Draw on the experience of everyone on the team.

"**"** "None of us is as smart as **all of us**"

# You're not alone...

None of us is as smart as all of us. The very nature of teams is that the team is bigger than any one individual; the leader's role is just that, one of leadership to guide the team through the continual stages of team development. No single individual has all the solutions and no one person can perform all the roles that make up a team. Right from the outset take the time to recognize that you have the opportunity to harvest many talents and past experiences and draw on deep experience from your team. Understand that your team has a wealth of knowledge and there is enormous value in drawing on the 'people resources' at your disposal. Through their inclusion and participation and by valuing their opinions and giving them ownership you are already harnessing the power of teams.

How many people are on your team 5, 10, 15, 30?

How many collective years of work experience do they have to draw on?

How many different salons have they collectively worked in?

## That's a lot of experience.

↑ Lesson: Understand "the power of we".

# Business's that are aligned get where they want faster...

By definition, a team is when every member shares the same vision and values, wants the same outcome and agrees on what it will take to get it. In my experience the key to this lays in employing the right people in the first place, as opposed to trying to change people once they are part of your team.

Frequently in the hair and beauty industry, the criteria for employing a team member is based solely on technical and creative skills and the superficial appearance of the applicant. In reality, it is the hidden and often less obvious attributes that will determine the 'fit' of the individual with the rest of the team and more importantly the 'fit' with the business vision, values and goals.

## How do you get that fit?

↑ Lesson: Employ people who already believe in your vision and values.

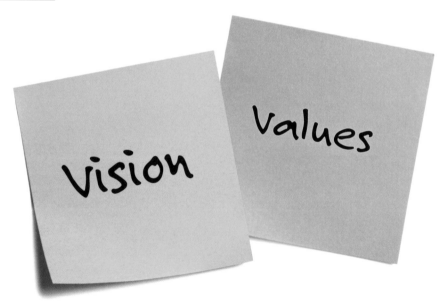

# Attitude is more important than skill...

When I first opened my salons my main criteria for employing people was skill level and appearance. Now, obviously both of those attributes are important, after all we are in the beauty business, so it helps if our own appearance measures up and that we look good and have the skills required to perform our job. However, just like they say the top three most important things when buying property are 'location, location, location,' when employing staff the top three things are 'attitude, attitude, attitude'. If you take nothing else from this book, please remember that.

## Skill is important, appearance is important but attitude is absolutely paramount.

{ When employing staff the top three things are 'attitude, attitude, attitude' }

You can train people to have better skills ...but only if they have the right attitude.

You can coach and help people with their appearance ...but only if they have the right attitude.

Think about it, if you were to list the characteristics of the worst team member they would probably look something like this...

Bad timekeeping, lazy, argumentative, dishonest, unmotivated, poor hygiene standards, too many days off 'ill', unprofessional, not a team player, grumpy ...etc, etc.

On the other hand, if you were to list the characteristics of the best team member they would probably look something like this...

Fun, professional, polite, helpful, creative, courteous, supportive, punctual, receptive, self motivated, team player, ambitious, proactive...etc, etc.

With both those lists, the worst team member and the best team member, what I have listed [and feel free to add more] are nearly all about 'attitudes'. You can teach people to have the skill but only if they have the right attitude.

↑ Lesson: The number one criteria to look for with people on your team is attitude. Skill is important, appearance is important but attitude is absolutely paramount.

"The most valued **attribute** of the people on your team is not their skill, or how much money they currently bring in... Their most valued attribute is the **attitude** they bring to work everyday."

# Every team needs a coach

You may not call them the coach, in fact, in a salon you probably don't. Maybe they are called 'Manager', 'Salon Co-ordinator or 'Team Leader' but regardless of the title the function or role of the coach is essentially the same. Being a good 'coach' is a mindset. That's a really important distinction to make whether you're a team member or the person with the responsibility of coaching others to be their best. The coach's role is to give feedback; some people are really open and receptive to feedback even when it is not something they particularly want to hear, at some level they are still able to recognise that feedback comes with the best intentions for the individual and ultimately the team.

Sometimes that feedback may be about 'negative behaviours' but don't assume that all coaching is about telling you what you are currently doing wrong, it is also about reinforcing and celebrating positive behaviours. That's what the function of coaching is… to tutor, teach, guide and to help someone to improve their performance and to hold them accountable for the results they get.

> The function of the coach is to help someone improve their performance

A good coach is someone who gets you to do, what you don't want to do, so you can become who you want to become.

The coach holds a team member accountable for skill improvement, behaviours and productivity regardless of whether they are personally more capable. For example, the coach of a Grand Slam tennis player, or top athlete may not be more capable as an athlete but they are more capable as a coach. In short, the skills of being a good coach are not necessarily the same as the skills required to do it, what ever 'it' is.

The skills of being a good coach are the skills of communication, observation, teaching and helping a team member identify and set their own goals and objectives. A coach ensures that those objectives are aligned with the business goals and guides a team member towards their achievement.

↑ Lesson: To reach your potential you need a coach. You are not always going to like the coach. You definitely won't always agree with them but you have to respect and cooperate with them in bringing about change.

# Are you coachable?

Regardless of your position on the team you need to be coachable. Being an ongoing learner is essential for your professional development in any field, as most of us have neither the objectivity or the time to learn everything through personal experience. Most of us need help to get there and that's only going to happen if you are coachable.

## So, the question is… are you coachable?

To be coachable means to be:

- Approachable…not defensive and aggressive
- Attentive…able to listen and focus on what is being said
- Receptive…to constructive criticism and feed back, not defensive
- Curious…seeking to learn and understand
- Objective…to be able to be detached and open minded about what is being said
- Trusting…in the motives of the coach and the process of coaching
- Mouldable…open minded, willing and able to accept change
- Confident…in your own abilities and not being afraid to try different ways

{ Being coachable means 'not having to be right' }

Being coachable means 'not having to be right'. Being coachable means you must actively listen with the intent to learn rather than to show what you know. To be coachable means to be modest and open minded, it means letting go of excessive pride and ego. Any team member that feels that they have arrived at perfection is probably failing. Even the team leader needs a coach. The best professionals in every industry, including the hair and beauty industry, at all levels require coaching to improve and they know it.

Are you coachable? inspired by Sam Parker at givemore.com

↑ Lesson: Being coachable means you must actively listen with the intent to learn, rather than show what you know. The people on your team need to be coachable.

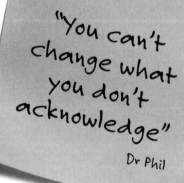

"You can't change what you don't acknowledge"

Dr Phil

"

"Above all, **don't fear** difficult moments. The best comes from them."

Rita Levi-Montalcini (1909 – )
Italian scientist, senator, Nobel Prize winner

# Staffroom terrorists:
# inspire them or fire them

Leaders or salon owners passionately believe that everything they do they do for the good of the business. Think about it, building and running a business is hard enough without having to fight with your own people. Salon owners already have enough of a challenge with the competition, with rising costs, the red tape of government, the banks, the tax department, landlords, product suppliers etc. You at least want the people on your team to be on your side!

Unfortunately the staffroom terrorist exists in many businesses and they do untold damage to everyone in the business, including themselves. Left unchecked they often think they are indispensable so they flex their muscles and over time become more and more demanding and destructive in the process. The problem is often exacerbated by the owner who also thinks that the terrorist is indispensable and so they feel held to ransom which makes it worse. Both are wrong, no one is ever indispensable, including you.

{ You can't change people, but they can change themselves }

Life really is too short to put up with people on your team who take all the joy out of coming to work. Whether you are a salon owner or an employee life is too short to keep having to accommodate the 'staffroom terrorist'. They are the individuals hell bent on ruining it for everyone. They are often slightly above average ability but also come with supercharged egos. They run amok and destroy team morale and poison everyone in their path. I occasionally still meet them in other people's salons, unfortunately I even employed the odd one over the years! They don't start out as terrorists but for whatever reason, left unchecked they are cancerous to the business and if you let them be, they will do untold damage in the process. You can't change people, but they can change themselves, if they want to. The problem is, often they don't want to.

Typically the staff room terrorist lacks the courage to do it on their own and open their own salon, they lack the respect to follow the leader and they lack the common sense to see that they are destroying their own reputation in the process. Often the leader has let them get out of control through some misguided idea that because they are a creative person they had to accept the superstar ego that goes with it. Nothing could be further from the truth.

# Why have they become like this?

Often it's because they think that's how they are meant to behave, so with no parameters they start to think of themselves as far more special than they actually are. They think that they are far more creative, far more important, far more valuable, far more of everything!

The real shame is that often if these people were managed properly from the outset they would respond really well but you have to be firm and you have to be consistent from day one to ensure they fulfill their true potential rather than the perceived potential of their own unchecked egos.

{ The 'staffroom terrorist' is like the worst sort of cancer to a business }

They may not always like it but hopefully they might recognise that they need it.

The really talented people in any industry are usually extremely professional, positive, very hard working, respectful of others and have humility. People like that are a real pleasure to be around.

↑ Lesson: The 'staffroom terrorist' is like the worst sort of cancer to a business and if left unchallenged they destroy careers and businesses in the process. If you have someone on your team who is a 'staffroom terrorist' challenge them on their constant negative input.

Everyone in your life is there for a reason

**"**

# "The bottom line in all of it is that, in life, it's all about people."

**Colin Powell (1937 – )**
**American statesman and**
**former U.S. Secretary of State**

# You get the team that you plan for...

Many of us spend more time at work than anywhere else, so creating and being part of a team of people that share common vision and values is essential. In doing so a team will work well together and respect and understand each other, it's in everyone's interest.

So how do we do that, how do we plan for that, where do we start? We start by asking…"what sort of team do you want to belong to?"

Perhaps we don't step back and ask that question often enough but that is the place to start, to constructively define the sort of team we want because we can't create what we haven't defined. We want to be part of a team and want to work in a business that makes us feel good about ourselves but what does 'feel good' mean?

We all want and need to feel connected, we all want to know that our lives matter and that we are making a contribution, we want to feel secure and know that we have the opportunity to grow. What you don't want is a team of people 'just like you'. I once heard it said that "building a team is like animals in a zoo, they're all animals but to get a good zoo you need variation". So, how do we first define and then create the team we want? What does it take to make that happen?

{ What sort of team do you want to belong to? }

The answers come from the questions. The questions that we need to ask and reflect on as a team because that will define and shape who we are as a team? Questions like:

• What sort of team do we want to belong to?
• What expectations do we have of each other?
• What opportunities are there for the team?
• What training is there for the team?
• What motivates the team as a team, and as individuals?
• How will the team be rewarded?
• What are the roles goals and responsibilities of the team?
• How will we measure performance on the team?
• How will we give feed back to the team?
• How will we celebrate on our team?

There is no 'right' or 'final' list of questions but asking the questions of yourselves as a team forces you to start defining what it is that you want as a team and that is the first step to making it happen.

↑ Lesson: You get the team that you plan for, so what sort of team is it you want? You can't create what you haven't defined.

**Checklist** Chapter 2:
# Who is on your team?

• As the manager it is your job to create a real sense of belonging on your team at an emotional not just a theoretical level.

• Understand that you can't do it alone; everyone on the team has a role to fulfil.

• A team has a collective consciousness, a 'synergy' where individuals think and act as one. You are building a 'Championship Team' not a 'Team of Champions.'

• Every team needs systems, structure and clearly defined roles goals and responsibilities if it is to operate in a consistent and predictable manner.

• Everyone on the team is unique and what they bring to the team is an invaluable contribution.

• For a team to reach its potential you need a coach. Are your team coachable?

• As the manager you need to understand the different motives, behaviours, needs and expectations of those on the team.

• Attitude is the number one criteria to look for when seeking team members

• Staffroom terrorists; inspire them or fire them

• You get the team that you plan for. What sort of team do you want to belong to? You can't create what you haven't defined.

# 3

# CREATING YOUR TEAM CULTURE

"

"Your team has a culture. I don't know if it is a **good** culture or a **bad** culture. I don't know if it works for you or against you. But, I do know that it exists."

# Define the 'team culture' or it will define you

Your team has a culture. I don't know if it is a good culture or a bad culture. I don't know if it works for you or against you. But, I do know that it exists.

- So where did it come from?
- Whose culture is it?
- How do we change it?

Most people who work in the hair and beauty industry are creative souls and they are good at designing the visual representation of the business ie what it looks like. However, just as it's important to design what it will look like, it is equally important to purpose-fully design the 'culture' of the business. That culture is how the business operates and reflects the standards, values, acceptable behaviours, habits, rituals and traditions of the business and the team.

*Define the Culture*

Taking the time to clearly define the culture of your team will pay dividends long term. Without absolute clarity your culture will be vague and open to interpretation, so it is important that you define your culture early and as your business grows you need to keep the team actively involved in evolving the culture.

Your culture must be committed to writing and actively shared through training, in this way your team members can bring YOUR culture alive. Until you have defined the culture of your team and written it down and people trained in what it is, and how to live it, it will depend on the individual, it will be their culture and at best it will be based on what they did where they previously worked.

↑ Lesson: Until you have defined the culture of your team and written it down and people trained in what it is, and how to live it, it will depend on the individual, it will be their culture and at best it will be based on what they did where they previously worked.

# The culture of teams...

Normally when you think about the word 'culture' you think of it in the context of a country and you would describe it in terms of their foods, music, traditions, religions, acceptable norms of behaviour, manners values.

When you go to a country you are immediately immersed into their way of life and experience the culture of the country as all encompassing. Think of the culture of a business in much the same way. The salon also has accepted norms of behaviour, shared values, beliefs, tone of communication and traditions etc and this is what determines the salon's culture. Likewise when you go into a salon you are immediately immersed in the culture of the business.

{ Culture is a lot about what you as a salon value as important }

Team work is a positive part of a business culture, in some salons there is no or little team work, in others it's a pervasive component of how the salon operates. Culture is a lot about what you as a salon value as important, not just from the perspective of creating a harmonious environment in which to work, but also from the perspective of making the business run as productively and efficiently as possible.

## So what are your team's most important values? What are your values as the leader? What are the most important values of your clients?

When you put answers to these questions you are starting to establish the values, the desirable behaviours, tone of communication and a systems of shared beliefs. This is what contrives to create the culture of your business...at least on paper.

↑ Lesson: Team work is a very positive part of a successful salon business and as the owner you need to consciously establish a culture of team work.

"The culture of **'team work'** is the result of the accepted standards, behaviours, rituals, values, beliefs, habits and expectations that exist within the team…"

# What is important to you and the rest of your team? What are your values?

Values are 'what we value'. Our values are quite simply 'the things that are important to us'. As an individual you might list your values or the 'things that are important to you' as things like having an affectionate loving relationship, family time, honest open communication, fun, entertaining friends, health and vitality, listening to great music. There is no right or wrong answer.

As an individual, your values define your personality and your character, whereas in a business shared values are one of the key things that define and underpin the team culture. So as a business...what are your values? What are the values of others on the team? Are they the same? For example, you might list 'training, punctuality, professionalism and fun' as values on your team.

> { Our Values are quite simply the things that are important to us }

They are all admirable values ...but not necessarily right for everybody. For example, imagine I am a 35 year old stylist working with you, that perhaps 15 years ago might have listed training as being important to me as 'a value.' But, now I no longer feel (rightly or wrongly) that I need to attend training and besides "I have children and I need to get home and get the dinner on. Training is no longer one of my values".

Or, another example, imagine I am a 23 year old stylist and really into the creative aspect of my work, "I'm an artist, and my art takes as long as it takes", while punctuality maybe a prioritised value to the owner and the client "the most important thing to me is perfection of my art! Punctuality is not one of my values".

In both of these examples it doesn't make me (as the stylist) right or wrong, I just have different values. In this example because I have different values to the owner and others on the team then in the immortal words from the movie Apollo 13... "Houston we have a problem".

There is no right or wrong list of values whether it is for an individual or a business but for a harmonious and successful team you need people who predominantly share the same values. Remember, it is easier to add people to your team who already share your values than it is to change someone's values but first you must define them.

As you can see in the above examples our values can and do change over time but part of what makes a team united and strong, is shared values. So it's important that you give serious thought in regard to your values and those of your team.

What are the real values of your business? The real values need to be just that REAL. As opposed to the 'nice, warm, fluffy values' that are written down by many businesses yet bear little resemblance to the daily demonstrated behaviours seen with clients or the team. Listing the company values can't just be something that was thought up in the marketing department as an essential box to tick on the business plan, it needs to be clear and it needs to be real.

In a business, when people are asked to list their values they will typically use words such as honesty, trust, respect, professionalism, teamwork, communication and training.

In the chart below I have listed 67 values, (feel free to add to the list) they are not right or wrong, they are simply a list of things that may or may not be important to you and your team. I am asking you to choose your top five. Choose them first in any order but to start with limit it to the five things that are the most important to your team.

| | | | |
|---|---|---|---|
| Accountability | Dependability | Happiness | Reliability |
| Achievement | Determination | Hard work | Rest |
| Acknowledgement | Discipline | Health | Results orientated |
| Ambition | Discretion | Honesty | Security |
| Assertiveness | Diversity | Honour | Service |
| Balance | Education | Humility | Speed |
| Being the best | Efficiency | Intelligence | Stability |
| Cleanliness | Enthusiasm | Integrity | Style |
| Commitment | Excellence | Leadership | Success |
| Community | Excitement | Love | Team work |
| Compassion | Fairness | Mastery | Thoughtfulness |
| Connection | Family | Originality | Tolerance |
| Continuous improvement | Focus | Passion | Trustworthiness |
| Contribution | Freedom | Productivity | Vision |
| Control | Fun | Professionalism | Vitality |
| Cooperation | Generosity | Profit | Wealth |
| Creativity | Growth | Pride | |

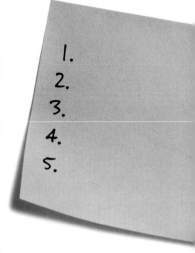

1.
2.
3.
4.
5.

Done? ...Now list them in order one to five with number one being the one word that is your number one value! The thing that is the most important to your team, the one thing (if there was to be only one) that is the most important to you.

I would do the exercise by yourself first and then do it with the rest of your team, ask them to individually list what they feel the top five values of the team are (or should be) and then discuss it and see if you can agree on a list and an order of priority.

It's good to involve all the team in this exercise and it's even better if they can all agree on the values of the team but the most important thing is that the owner is happy with the list because the team may come and go but the business will still be there and it needs to 'stand' for something.

Listing the words is just the beginning, it is not enough to just list the words because words alone mean different things. For example, if in my list of values I wrote the words 'team work' you may draw a different meaning from that value than me.

In a work environment team work means different things to different people. Team work, professionalism, respect etc all have differing definitions, depending on who you talk to. Each of these words is open to individual interpretation. The end result is that although everyone pays lip service to acknowledging that team work is important, they all have different definitions of what team work entails. They probably bring their own definition with them based on where they worked before and they may or may not be a good reference point. What you need to do is take the time to define the criteria by which team work and every value on your list is to be defined in the context of your business. For example:

{ The team may come and go but the business will still be there }

Team work:
*"Everyone who works here is part of our team and contributes to their own success, the success of the team and the overall success of the business.*

*As a team member, I will always ask for help should I need it and I am here to assist the rest of the team in any way I can.*

*As a team we believe everyone is here to assist the rest of the team in any way they can as the clients satisfaction supersedes any individual needs regardless of title/age/seniority*

*No one leaves the salon at the end of the day or sits in the back room during the day unless the salon is spotless."*

Now no one is in any doubt about what team work means in this business.

I am not suggesting that that is the right definition of team work, there isn't a right or wrong definition, but I believe it is important to define what it means to your team, not with vague feel good fluff but with defined actions and expected behaviours.

Another example is the word 'professional' which is often a value that salons feel obliged to choose but what does it mean to you and your team?

**Professionalism:**

*"As a professional it is important that all of our actions and communications are performed with the utmost attention to detail, care and integrity and are in-line with the company's core values.*

*We do everything we can to ensure that we run on time.*

*Our personal appearance, cleanliness, hygiene and grooming standards are always on show and must consistently be of the highest level.*

*Everyone has to have a full compliment of required salon tools and must keep them clean and in good working order.*

*No one is to borrow another stylist tools without permission."*

Now no one is in any doubt about what 'professionalism' means to this team.

Again I am not saying that this is the correct definitions of professionalism, what I am saying is that they are 'the' definitions of my imaginary team and give me a framework on which to build a team culture. Words are open to individual interpretation and so it's important to take the time to define their meaning and context in your business. It is only in this way that you really communicate the meaning and the expected corresponding behaviour.

{ As a team member I will always ask for help }

# Have you defined what values are important to both you and the rest of your team?

If you asked your team, what values would they say the business currently represents?

While nobody wants to work with people who are selfish, dishonest and miserable or people who are lazy or bullies, sometimes these destructive attributes unfortunately creep into the workplace.

↑ Lesson: Taking the time to define what is important to you and the rest of your team (your core values and beliefs) is taking a major step in defining a culture for all to see and work by.

# Teams need an agreed code of conduct...

What is a code of conduct? Whether you call them rules, standards, behaviours, responsibilities, agreements or a charter, we all need a code of conduct in order to function and not have confusion, chaos and anarchy. All around us are 'rules' or an acceptable 'code of conduct'; from the rules of war, government, traffic, sport or religion and so on.

These rules give us a structure in which to operate, they define the parameters and behaviours that we are expected to adhere to. Rules also give us a sense of control and security because they reduce the fear of the unknown and create a framework on which to base our daily lives and guide our behaviours.

> Rules give us a structure in which to operate

As a team you need a clearly defined set of expectations that exists as part of a job description and 'policy and procedures' manual but over and above that you should develop an 'agreed code of conduct' – think of it as your ten commandments that focus on mutual expected behaviours. This agreed code of conduct gives everyone on the team clear direction, focus and purpose. It supports the company standards and values and leaves no doubt in everyone's mind as to what behaviours they are expected to exhibit and will be held accountable for.

For some people perhaps the word 'rules' has a negative connotation, so consider another terminology. I like the words 'agreement' or 'code of conduct', as they imply positive behaviours that we can all agree and act on. You decide the terminology that you feel is a best fit to your company culture.

Regardless of what you choose to call it, the 'code of conduct' should be a positive expression, a summary of your company beliefs and ethos' that will define acceptable standards and behaviours

What are the rules our team need to live by?

The following are some of the points that you may wish to include in your 'Code of Conduct':

- Being on time; the importance of punctuality
- Being willing to support the company vision
- Speaking supportively and with good intentions
- Always allowing another person their point of view
- There is no failure except the failure to participate
- Make agreements and stick to them
- Be effective and efficient with your resources and time
- Always aim for a win:win situation
- Treat others as you would like them to treat you
- Respect each other
- Focus on what works; always look at the positive in people and situations
- If you're not sure, check and trust your intuition
- Be open to change. Be prepared to try, be constructive.

The 'code of conduct' will be a guide as you align everyone on your team.

{ There is no failure except the failure to participate }

Businesses that are aligned, get where they want to go faster and so do the individuals in them. That's win:win.

The 'code of conduct' inspired by Blair Singer.

↑ Lesson: Every team needs a 'code of conduct', a clear description of acceptable standards and behaviours. This agreed 'code of conduct' gives everyone on the team clear direction, focus and a purpose.

# What destroys a team culture?

I once did some work with a team of people where there seemed to be nothing but disharmony.

I started my training session by asking; "What it is that destroys a team culture?" and started to list their responses on a flip chart...

Poor management. No clear job description. No common vision. No clarity of expectations. Negative attitudes. Destructive criticism. Unprofessional behaviour. No team work.No communication. Not taking responsibility. Choosing to not be involved. Selfishness, Not sharing. Not celebrating success. Theft. Lack of defined culture. No personal or salon goals. No incentives. Ulterior motives. No respect for each other. Violence. Intimidation. Bossiness. Harassment. Lack of trust. Power games. Lack of honesty. People who think they're above others. Choosing to not change. Misunderstanding. Not wanting to understand. Stubbornness. Buck passing. Lack of guidance. Sloppiness. Lack of enthusiasm. Lack of appreciation for each other. Lack of training. Expectations not met. Over promised under delivered. Poor health. Boyfriend's/girlfriend's/husbands/wives/kids/family. Lack of involvement. Drama. Tears. Not handling emotions. No support. Inconsiderate behaviour. Not dealing with stress. Lack of confidence. Apathy. Militant expectations. Overworked/underworked. Put downs. Underpaid. Tension. Drugs. Alcohol. Cigarette smokers. Gossip. Constant absenteeism. Too busy. Negative compounding culture. Spoilt. Poor morale. Whiners tolerated. Poor self esteem. Poor self image. Lack of commitment. Not getting breaks. Backstabbing. Sabotage. Lack of tolerance. The wrong employees. Overstaffed. No meetings to voice opinions. Unnecessary rules. Bitchiness. Too much focus on what's wrong. Not focusing on what's right. Bitterness. Cultural differences. No follow through. Negative communication. Different agendas. Poor leadership. No policy and procedures. Uncooperative. Us and them mentality. Mismatched personalities. Frustration. Not following procedures. Lack of accountability. Trouble makers 'stirring the pot'. Conflict not resolved. Unofficial leaders. No confrontation. Too many chiefs not enough Indians. Prejudice. Sexism. Lost interest. Lost passion. Unnecessary hierarchy. Snobbery. People that lack courage and are afraid to leave. The list could have gone on!

{ The leader has to be decisive }

That is their list, I have edited the list down but I originally thought they would come up with a list of perhaps half a dozen points but they came up with 130 points 'that destroy a team culture.' This was a group of people that were completely obsessed with focusing on the negative, all they could ever see was what was wrong and they wallowed in every minute of it!

The points on this list are to a business what cancer is to the human body, left unchallenged they will systematically destroy the business from within and it is the job of everyone on the team to understand that what you have as a culture doesn't just happen ...it is the result of what everyone does and doesn't do.

↑ Lesson: What ever you focus on you get, everyone is responsible for the culture that exists on the salon team. Above all, the leader has to be decisive and not be afraid to take charge. If you permit it, you promote it.

# What are some tangible things to do that will create a positive team culture?

### Induction process
One of the key components in ensuring new team members understand your culture is to have a formal induction process with each team member before they start. The induction needs to cover everything about the business, including how you have a strong culture of 'teamwork' to ensure that they are in no doubt about the fact that "this is how we do it here".

### Lead from the front
Be first to demonstrate team work; pick up a broom, tidy the staffroom, and offer to help someone who's running behind. Look for ways to serve and help other team members, from offering to shampoo a client if they are running behind, to offering to get lunch for others if they are running late. Actively demonstrate the behaviours you want to see in your team ie get someone else's clients a coffee or magazine, help all the clients with their coats and bags, stay back and help clean up.

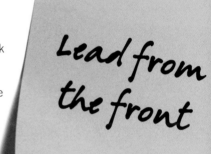

### Mentoring
Match up team members that need support to their peers with complimentary strengths.

### Develop your ten points of culture
Identify your top ten points of culture as your company's values and express your thoughts on each in writing. Your list might include things like: team work, fun, training, communication, gratitude and honesty.

For example on communication you might write something like:

### Communication
Most frustrations stem from a communication issue. As we grow as a company we are constantly re-evaluating our systems of communication to improve the work environment for everyone. As individuals we need to always communicate with each other and our clients in a professional, respectful and positive manner at all times.

↑ Lesson: Define your culture; nurture and protect it always.

# If you talk 'team' …
# you must reward the 'team'

## Do you talk team but reward the individual?

That's what many salon owners do…they talk! "Team this, team that, and team the other." But in reality, all the reward, training, and feed back is aimed at the individual. I'm not saying that individuals shouldn't be rewarded and given individual training and feed back, of course they should be. But if you really want to set up a team culture that is more than just a buzz word it requires a more holistic approach.

{ What goals do you want the team to achieve this week? }

First, you have to start by setting some team goals and objectives then you need a strategy to turn them into reality. What goals do 'you' want the team to achieve this week, this month, this year? What goals do the 'team' want to achieve this week, this month, this year?

Team goals
In what areas should you and your team be setting goals? For me, there are four key elements.
1. Team productivity goals. For example: what weekly salon performance indicators should you measure and set goals in?
   • What weekly total client count as a team?
   • What weekly total service revenue as a team?
   • What weekly retail revenue as a team?
   • What weekly percentage of all clients should have colour?
   • What weekly percentage of all clients should rebook their appointment?

2. Team creative goals. Many of your team will be motivated and inspired by goals that fulfil their creative needs.
   • What shows or seminars do you want to attend or participate in as a team?
   • What awards do you want to win or enter as a team?
   • What other creative goals could your team have?

3. Team learning goals. Everyone on your team will be at different stages of their career development but everyone needs to be a continual learner.
   • What new skills or knowledge do you as a team want to learn?
   • What hairdressing skills would you like to learn as a team?
   • What non hairdressing skills would you like to learn as a team?

4. Team fun goals. In many cases you will spend more time with your team than with your family and loved ones, so it's important that you have fun at work.
  - As a team what fun things do you want to do?
  - What fun things do you want to see as a team?
  - Where do you want to go to as a team for fun?

Once you have defined and set the team goals you have to follow up with relevant team training.

Team training
You can't set team goals and expect them to just happen. To give the goal the best chance of success you need to make sure the team have had the best possible training.

The goals you have set, will determine what training is required. As well as your own observations as to what skills the team lack, ask the team what training they feel they need.

Team work
What specific mentoring and practical team work do you need to see happening to make the team goals a reality?

Team feedback
Achieving team goals is all about team results and the team need feed back on the results they are getting as a team. What systems and processes do you have in place to give the team the feedback they need?

Finally, how are you going to reward the team and celebrate the team achievements?

Team rewards or celebrations
What rewards can you give the team for achieving the team goals?
  - You could split a bonus equally between all the team members
  - You could buy morning tea for the team
  - Pay for the team to attend an industry event, i.e. a show or awards event
  - Take the team out for dinner
  - Take the team for an overnight stay at a country retreat
  - Take the team to attend a concert together
  - Take the team out for a massage or manicure
  - Take the team out to a 'big game'

what team rewards could you instigate?

↑ Lesson: If you talk team, reward team. Develop a holistic approach that includes; team goals, team training, team work, team feedback and team rewards and celebrations.

# Passion: the noble emotion

Passion is often an overused word in hairdressing but PASSION is a very important word and an essential ingredient in your success and that of your team.

## So what is passion?

Everybody uses the phrase, everyone wants it but what exactly is it?

{ Passion is a distinct strong and noble emotion }

## Is it pride, determination, hunger, enthusiasm, conviction, commitment, courage, love...?

## Or is it all of the above?

Passion is a distinct strong and noble emotion and you know it when you see it, When you're in the presence of someone who is passionate about their work, they leave you with a sense of enthusiasm a sense of wanting to be around them. In their presence they make you more of who you are and they make you see who you could be. They make you feel more alive.

A passionate leader is like a magnet that draws everyone towards achievement of the highest standard. With passion people start to forget all the reasons that hold them back from achieving at a higher level because passion brings out the best in people. Passion is the thing that keeps you going when all others have stopped.

↑ Lesson: Usually the people who win are the people who want it the most! So how bad do you want it/need it? What will you sacrifice to get it? What will you go through to achieve it?

It's passion that makes the difference

# How do we manifest 'passion', not just within ourselves but others?

## How do you manifest more passion?

I don't really have a definitive answer but I do know that beyond a shadow of a doubt that passion is contagious, so we must develop a mindset and culture of passion in our business and as the leader that starts with you.

I do know that no one owes it to you. You have to cultivate it yourself; it is a choice and you either decide to be passionate or not."

One of the great things about the hair and beauty business is that the seeds of passion are everywhere in our industry, you need only attend a show or a seminar or look at all of creative awards entries to see pure unadulterated passion for hair is alive and well. We need to develop that passion as a driving force in our business. We need to extend that passion to applying a level of pride and excellence in everything we do, from the cleanliness of the salon and the level of customer service to the shows and beautiful images that many of us aspire to produce.

> { I know that beyond a shadow of a doubt that Passion is contagious }

What are some practical things you can do to increase the amount of passion that your team exhibit?

**Lead by example**
If you want to see passion in your team, you need to set a good example because passion is contagious; create a positive environment and don't accept less from yourself and than you do from your team.

**Have a zero tolerance to negativity**
Negativity, whether your own or from those around you is corrosive to passion, it eats away and destroys it if you let it. Decide to have zero tolerance on negativity in your team. If you don't like it, do something positive about it ...or leave.

**Everyone helps create a positive environment**
Everyone on the team has a responsibility to create a positive environment on the team, through their words and actions in order to be a force for good.

**Dream big dreams, be ambitious**
Passion fuels ambition, don't be afraid to dream the big dreams.
In the words of the late Steve Jobs CEO and Co-founder Apple Inc
"Let's make a dent in the universe" .

**Do passion**
Passion is an attitude, so what do you do when you are passionate?
What do you say? How do you say it? What do you think about
when you are passionate? How do you move when you are
passionate? The more you understand what you do when you do
passionate, the more you can manifest more passion!

**Have balance in your life?**
Passion is energy, you cannot be passion personified 24/7 you also
have to have a balance in your life. So plan time to chill, time with
loved ones and time alone to recharge your own batteries.

**Stay fit healthy**
You can't be passionate if you are not looking after yourself. You
need good fresh food, rest, fresh air, water, exercise ...you don't
need alcohol, substance abuse, a diet of processed food, a lack of
sleep and a packet of Marlborough!

**Positive empowering affirmations/thoughts**
You can choose your thoughts, so why not choose uplifting,
inspiring, positive thoughts. "As you think, so shall you become."

**Staff library**
Assemble a staff resource library of empowering books tapes and
DVD's.

**Internal and external competitions**
Bring out the competitive spirit in your team by competing with
each other and others in your industry.

**Attend external non-industry seminars**
Look at those outside your industry for inspiration and new ways of
thinking and acting.

↑ Lesson: Passion is the thing that keeps you going when all
others have stopped, passion is the thing that makes you detail
obsessed, passion is what keeps you together in moments of
crisis, passion is what sets you and your team apart from the
rest. Decide to be passionate.

{ "As you think so you shall become" }

# The passionate leader

When the qualities of leadership and responsibility are combined with the emotional quality of passion, people respond.

Passion is contagious so when the leader is passionate it attracts, inspires and motivates a team to perform at their optimum. Passion is that special ingredient that has carried many an individual or team to victory, it is the 'X Factor', the undefinable quality that pushes people to perform at another level.

In sport you often see a team that is technically and theoretically superior but they come up against an opponent with more passion, more pride and more commitment. In other words, they stand up and take ownership of it. That sense of synergy is the kind of passion that ignites and inspires people to perform at a personal best and it is as relevant in business as it is on the sports field. When you create that synergy in a business it takes your team and their productivity to another level.

↑ Lesson: The passion of the leader is the spark that ignites the team.

If you're the leader it starts with you

# Creating your team culture

- As the manager you need to define the team culture, or it will define itself and it won't be what you want or what the business needs.

- What are your values? What is important to you and your team? As the manager you need to define your values as they will be the bedrock on which your culture is built.

- Does everyone on your team have a definitive understanding of team work in your salon?

- Every team needs a code of conduct to define the parameters and behaviours that they are expected to adhere to.

- Culture is easily destroyed, everyone has a responsibility to live it but above all, as the manager it is your job to define, nurture and guard the company culture.

- If you talk 'team', you must look for ways to reward 'the team'.

- Consciously look for ways to develop passion in the team but above all lead by example.

# TRAINING:
# BUILDING A CULTURE OF EXCELLENCE

"I learned very early on that you can be very, very **talented** but if you don't take care of your talent, it can go away. It's like a big baby. It needs to be fed."

Annie Leibovitz (1949 – )
American photographer

# Training, learning, upskilling, practice...

If you want to be good at something you have got to practice it, not once or twice but repeatedly...and then do it some more. Practice, training, learning ...whatever you want to call it never stops and when it does, so do you. If you are in any doubt about the validity of that statement just look at the great footballers, the great ballerinas, or musicians, or artists, or presenters ...or hairdressers. Training, learning, looking for distinctions, a seeking a better way of doing it, it never stops!

I have a fond memory of a time in 1980 when I was in staff training at Vidal Sassoon London and as a very rare treat the day was being taken by the International Creative Director of the time Christopher Brooker. I was much in awe of the man and wanted desperately to show him how clever I thought I was. The problem was that the only victim I mean model, that I could get was a little old lady that resembled the Queen mother. Resigned to the fact that I had to cut her hair, I decided to get through it as quickly as I could and planned that I would then go back to reception and get someone with great hair, someone more open minded about change, someone gorgeous and preferably someone under the age of 85. I anticipated that I would have my little old lady client shampooed, cut, blow dried and out the door in under 45 minutes. The problem was that Christopher had other ideas.

*"We are what we repeatedly do. Excellence then is not an act but a habit"*

*Aristotle (384 BC – 322 BC)*

Being the absolute perfectionist that he was Christopher made me go over it and over it, section by section, again and again. It was in my eyes beyond perfection and what I had thought would take 45 minutes turned into more than four and a half hours! When I had finally finished the cut and then blow dried her hair, he checked it one last time. Smiling he turned to me and said "Fantastic! Now what I want you to do is take the lady to the backwash, give her hair one light shampoo and cut it again, this time take no more than a quarter of an inch off but make it look like it couldn't have been done anywhere else but at Vidal Sassoon!"

I thought he was joking ...He wasn't.

Interestingly, this time it did take 45 minutes ...and I learnt yet more distinctions the second time around.

{ There is a difference between looking and seeing. }

## Perfection is in the detail.

There is a difference between looking and seeing.

↑ **Lesson: To be master of anything requires practice, repetition, feedback, humility, perseverance and an obsessive attention to detail.**

# Training needs to be a system

To build an ongoing culture of excellence requires a system. Without a system standards become dependent on the individuals and individuals come and go. With a system a culture of excellence becomes standardised, repeatable, measurable and scaleable.

Every salon should have within their budget a training component. Good education can require a considerable investment but the right things, with the right people, will pay huge dividends.

As someone once said "What if I spend all this money training people and they leave?" To which the response was "What if you don't and they stay?"

Your training program needs to start at the beginning, before any employee has contact with clients, suppliers or the rest of the team.

↑ Lesson: Training is to ensure standards and standards need consistency. In order to get those consistent standards the training and the processes need to be systemised.

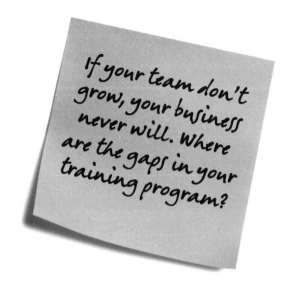

If your team don't grow, your business never will. Where are the gaps in your training program?

# Induction training system

## Training starts with a thorough induction.

When you take on a new team member regardless of their age, experience or position, they need 'induction training' to ensure that from day one, they get off on the right foot. Every employee needs to understand the company background, it's past history, present situation and future goals. Every employee must understand their job description and role expectations and their place in the team. Every employee must truly internalise the values of your company to understand that 'this is the way you do things here'.

{ Every employee must understand their job descritption }

As the manager, it is not necessarily your job to personally deliver every induction but it is your job to develop a system that covers all the content and includes a series of checklists to ensure that no matter who delivers the training everything is covered, agreed and signed off on. It is only by giving everyone a thorough induction that you can reasonably hold people accountable for their performance.

How long should 'induction training' take? How long is a piece of string? It takes as long as it takes. Without a thorough and positive induction your best hope is that your new employee will behave just as they did in their previous position, with their previous employer. If you want to create a team that reflects your business then you must establish a clear induction training as every team member is employed.

## For those people who say, 'I don't have the time!' Really? You don't have the time not to!

# Delivering 'the experience' training system

You are not just selling a product or service. As I frequently say "They can get the haircut elsewhere". What you are competing on now more than ever before is not just the haircut and colour, but the experience. That's a total experience for the client from how you answer the phone, greet them on arrival, present refreshments, to how you deal with complaints and implement change and so on.

{ It's not just the haircut and colour, but the experience }

After years of working with clients we often subconsciously develop 'best practice' ways of how we expect things done, it's who 'you have become'.

If you expect others to adopt the same standards and approach it is unrealistic to expect them to know 'how' without being trained in the 'why' of the process. As the manager your job is to develop training systems that cover every facet of 'the client experience'.

When developing training systems, they don't have to be just the 'written word'. Where possible utilise, photographs, video and role playing exercises to get the message across. Every element must detail a 'best practice' standard for your business and without a system and the training that accompanies it you are relying on common sense and people having the same standards as you do.

what you are selling is not just a product or service, you are selling an experience and it needs to be consistent

# Product knowledge training system

In every industry there are specific products that you use in the course of your job that you need to have a thorough technical and practical understanding of. Not only from a safety perspective but also the opportunity to retail professionally prescribed brands to increase revenue and provide clients with professional advice that deliver the ideal home hair care maintenance program.

Develop a training system for your team in conjunction with your professional product suppliers to ensure all your team have a complete and up to date understanding of the products they use.

# Health and safety training system

Obviously you want to provide a safe environment for both your team and clients when they are in your work place. As the manager, it is certainly in your interest to do so as failing to train your team in the correct 'health and safety' practices in the workplace can be a very expensive mistake. Not just through lost productivity if people are off work injured, (or worse) but in the event that clients or team members come to harm you could find yourself in a very costly legal nightmare.

Admittedly, in today's workplace, in my opinion, there are many examples where 'health and safety' has gone mad but regardless of opinion it is the law and the last thing you want to do, (or have time to do) is to be bogged down in court by a health and safety mistake. Health and safety laws vary from country to country, in some cases there are literally no laws, in others it has become so excessively over regulated as to be bordering on the ridiculous.

Regardless of where you live, if you don't have a 'legal responsibility' you certainly have a 'moral' responsibility to look after your clients and staff members while they are on your property. Take responsibility for finding out the health and safety laws in your country and provide the appropriate training and resources for all your team.

It may not be fun, it may not be creative and exciting but it is essential.

# Technical and creative training system

In the hair and beauty business so much of what we do revolves around the technical and creative ability of our team. Having a solid foundation in the technical and creative skills is essential as is a commitment to ongoing training to ensure that everyone on the team remains abreast with the current trends and techniques. As a business, it is a definite weakness if the client is beholden to just one individual having the skill to deliver the product or service that you have.

In order for the technical and creative aspect to be consistently of a certain standard and be able to be reproduced by others on your team you need to develop a training program that takes everyone through the same techniques, so that it is not reliant on the individual but on the training.

{ You have to stand for something }

In short, "You have to stand for something" and it needs to be repeatable.

# Personal development training system

## "We are not our job. We have a job but we are not our job."

No matter how much you love what you do, you are not 'what' you do. As a business owner with staff, if you create opportunities to develop not just 'the hairdresser' but 'the complete person' within your business they will probably stay with you longer as opposed to feeling that the only way to 'grow' is to leave and look for opportunities elsewhere.

Over the years I have seen many diverse training programs in salons including public speaking, make-up, yoga, pilates, financial management, cooking, clothes styling, conflict management, art classes, photography and presentation skills.

All of them in some way contribute to the personal development, happiness and well-being of the people on the team. Although there are no guarantees, a happy team is more likely to be a loyal team and a happy team is more likely to be a productive team.

# Management and leadership training system

Your business is a reflection of you, and if you don't grow, your business never will. It's easy to get into a situation where all your investment is in developing others, you need training too! Every year you should invest time and money in your own personal and professional development both technically and creatively in order to develop a diverse range of business and personal skills.

{ Your business is a reflection of you }

As well as all the obvious industry based training opportunities, look outside of the norm and consider expanding your skills by seeking education in some of the following areas: conflict resolution, negotiating, interviewing, IT, time management, social media, copy writing, photography, property, cash flow management, coaching, budgets.

↑ Lesson: You need to have a training system so that the standards and processes that you have can be repeated again and again, consistently and in every area of business to the same standards and no matter who is doing it.

If you don't grow your business never will

# Training, final thoughts

**Modular learning...**

Developing your own training program is not an easy task and in many cases unfortunately they don't exist in any structured form. As a salon owner/manager with the increasingly high cost of employing people it is more important than ever that your team becomes productive as quickly as possible.

Having a structured training program with clearly defined goals and objectives to be reached within specific time frames, gives everyone clarity and understanding of what is expected of them. Breaking the training needs and objectives into a series of modules that include individual units within each module, helps create a logical flow of what needs to be covered and when.

**Learning styles. Mix it up...**

We all learn in different ways. Some of us are what is termed 'visual learners' meaning we process and take in information more through what we see. Others take in and process information more through what we hear and are termed 'auditory learners'. Finally, we have 'kinaesthetic' learners that are people who learn more through what they feel and experience. Although all of us learn through utilising all three learning modes, I suspect, that as a group those in the hair and beauty business tend to learn primarily through visual and kinaesthetic modes.

## The question is "Does your training program reflect that?"

Some people will learn just by watching you and observing how you do it, i.e. watching you with a client. Others need the explanation that goes with it, i.e. watching a demonstration or a DVD, and the final group won't really learn unless 'they' are actually doing it, i.e. a hands on workshop or role playing exercises.

Once you are aware of how different people learn it becomes a lot easier to mix up the training using theory, practical, demonstrations, workshops, video, audio etc. This not only makes the training more fun but you also speed up the progress and understanding of those you are teaching.

## Models and Mannequins

All of my training as a hairdresser from a technical and creative perspective took place on live models. However looking back on it, teaching and learning 'technique' especially at the beginning, can be done equally as well and perhaps better, on a mannequin head without being distracted by the person and all their 'needs'. I think the best way to teach and learn technique is to first focus on mastering the technique. Mastering technique allows you to forget about the fact that your model has to get back to work, or her dad won't like it, or her hair is too fine, or she can't have it like that for school, or she's trying to grow it for her wedding etc etc ...all of that will come later, master the fundamental technique first.

Once the technique on a mannequin has been mastered there is then the confidence to adapt technique and creativity to suit the needs of the individual.

{ We all learn in different ways }

## The Generation Game

Without doubt there are different needs and expectations in the learning and teaching styles for different generations. I'll often hear people of my generation talk about how it was "when they were training" but that was then, this is now. The hair and beauty industry has always had a high number of 16-25 year olds and that generation has always been at the forefront of change.

We live in a world of instant gratification, information and knowledge is just a 'click' away. Understandably the thought of taking 3-4 years doing an apprenticeship and spending years cleaning up, making tea and doing the laundry etc is perhaps not as appealing as it once was. Without doubt, advances in technology have made learning anything more readily accessible and therefore faster but, there is often now an unrealistic expectation for many that they want results NOW!. There is no regard for the fact that thousands of hours of practice and self discipline go into mastering anything.

There is a great book called 'Outliers' by Malcolm Gladwell that talks about it taking 10,000 hours (that's five years of 40 hour weeks) to master anything. Malcolm offers examples of so called 'over night successes' from The Beatles to Bill Gates investing 10,000 hours before achieving anything.

If there are massive differences among different generations and subsequently in the workplace, then to get the best out of people it's essential to understand each generation, and adapt training, communication and management style around them.

There have always been individuals with different needs, values, ideas, ways of communicating and getting things done. However all employees need inspiring leadership, a balance of authority and support. They all need to feel valued and respected, and feel that they are making a meaningful contribution. What the next generation brings in return is a fresh way of thinking and looking at the world and hopefully a level of enthusiasm, energy and passion to bring about positive change.

### Acknowledge achievement

As your team members progress from one stage to the next in their training, make sure you take the opportunity to acknowledge their achievement. It can be as simple as announcing at the team meeting that a team member has passed their test or graduated to the next stage. The power of that peer recognition, acknowledgement and round of applause from their colleagues is not to be underestimated.

{ Acknowledge their achievment }

### To pay, or not to pay?

In many countries the hairdressing industry has long had a cultural tradition of training being unpaid and conducted 'out of hours'. There is little point in talking about what happened when you were a boy/girl, as nobody is really interested. It's always a contentious issue when brought up at seminars and the legalities vary from country to country but in most western countries it is now often the case that legally you are required to pay for all training.

I meet many people that have secured signed waivers saying that the staff agree to attend training on a voluntary basis, however I also meet people who say that in their experience in court those waivers are not binding. Put it this way: "In ten years time do you think more salons or less salons will be paying staff to attend training?"

I think we all know the answer to that one.

**Workbook**

Many years ago I was advised to invest in a good hardcover journal and bring it with me to every seminar I attended, I took the advice and I have done it ever since. The result is that I have hard cover journals that are a collection of all the seminars I have attended over the years. I still use them today as a valuable resource.

As someone who presents seminars for a living, it always amazes me that people turn up without a pen or paper and still expect to retain the days information. The reality is that we forget at least 50% of what we hear within four hours whereas writing information down, even if you never read it increases retention dramatically.

{ We forget at least 50% of what we hear within four hours }

So invest in a good hardcover journal, perhaps give one to all of your team and insist that they take it to every training event so that all their notes and diagrams are kept together in one place.

## "You never conquer the mountains. You only conquer yourself"

Jim Whitaker, climber Mount Everest

Invest in a hardcover journal and bring it to every seminar

# Training Systems

- As the manager, for standards to be predictable and consistent, you need to develop a documented training system that covers every area of your business.

- Training programs need to cover: induction, delivering the customer experience, product knowledge, health and safety, technical and creative, personal development, as well as management and leadership training.

- Develop a modular training program that also tracks the learner's goals and progress in real time.

- Not everyone learns the same so 'mix it up' from models to mannequins, theory to practical, live demonstrations to YouTube workshops and CD's, the more mediums you use, the more fun and inspiring the learning will be.

- Integrate your training program with your product supplier.

- Never let a chance go by to acknowledge and celebrate the achievements of your team.

- The trainer or coach is a very influential role in your salon, choose wisely.

- Compile and keep all your notes together in a binder or journal.

# COMMUNICATION

# You cannot, not communicate

Everything we say and do, is communicating something. Equally, everything we 'don't do and say' is communicating something. You cannot, not communicate.

Think about any relationship, usually the problems are caused by, or certainly exacerbated by communication. Fortunately, they are also sorted out by communication. As part of a team you have to commit to being part of a cycle of open honest communication. That doesn't mean you have carte blanche to ignore peoples feelings but on a team you need to be able to communicate openly and candidly. You won't always like what is said but if you're unable to have meaningful conversations with the people on your team, go and get some professional help. It's not personal, it's business and sometimes egos get bruised.

{ Everything we say and do is communicating something }

## Communication in all its forms is what connects the team.

From having team meetings, notice boards, mission and vision statements, goals, targets, social media, conflict resolution strategies, policy manuals, weekly reports, KPI's and on and on the list goes. Your role as the manager is to create a culture of communication and develop the communication systems so that everyone on the team is contributing to effective and efficient communication.

↑ Lesson: In a team, or for that matter any relationship, most of your frustrations stem from a communication issue so we all need to ensure that we make all our communication effective and positive.

Most frustrations stem from a communication issue

"The **real conversations** that are required to sustain a relationship are easily recognised. They are the ones that keep getting put off for another day."

# What makes the team relationship work?

Every one of us is in a number of relationships – some good, some not so good.

Those relationships might be with your husband, wife, boyfriend, girlfriend, son, daughter, mother, father, colleagues, employer, employee's etc and like all relationships they are complex at the best of times,

A team is many things but essentially a team is a series of relationships and these relationships can be complicated and fraught with challenges as they evolve.

So what makes that team relationship 'work'?

Not just your team but any team. Think of great sporting teams, or bands, great marriages, businesses, families, political parties, they are all teams and as such are in a continuous state of flux.

There isn't a finite list of ingredients that make for a good relationship but this is a good start.

Honest open communication, Compatibility, Loyalty, Trust, Leadership, Fun, Vision, Common goals, Risk, Attention to detail, Pride, Passion, Friendship, Recognition, Reward, Rules, Practice/training, Co-operation, Commitment.

These are not just words, this is the glue…a way of thinking and living that makes relationships work and we need these attributes in our business to make them work to the maximum.

Look at the list and ask yourself, "What do I" (yes, you!) Need to learn about communication, loyalty, trust, leadership etc. On a scale of 1-10 how would you rate yourself in each of these, how would you rate the rest of your team? Where do you need to focus your attention?

↑ Lesson: A team is a series of relationships, the attributes that make for good relationships out of work are mostly the same attributes that make for a good team dynamic in work.

# When a relationship isn't working you have two choices...

I often meet business owners who have poor or no communication with one or two members of the team and after several attempts to address the situation they have usually given up trying. That is when the real problems start to set in, which usually results in an 'us and them' mentality, lack of trust, a lack of teamwork and a slow destructive decline in morale. Problems in your team are like problems in any relationship, if you are in a 'relationship' and you are not happy, you have two choices...

## Do nothing or Do something

If you choose to 'do nothing', in time it may get better or it may get worse.

Occasionally time can be a great healer and sometimes allows the emotion to go out of things and issues can then be easier to deal with. However, if at some stage it is not dealt with then long term it will usually get worse, the issues will fester over time until they rear their head again when the occasion suits.

> { Occasionally time can be a great healer }

If you choose to 'do something' make it something positive to bring about positive change, confront the issues, get them out in the open and look for positive solutions. Acknowledge that you may well be at least partly at fault but it's not about laying blame and justification, it's about finding a positive solution.

The important thing is not to give up. That's not always easy as like in any relationship communication and 'effort' has to come from both sides, when it's a one sided attempt to solve the problem and move forward it will usually result in a stale mate.

But a 'stalemate' in any relationship isn't a solution and a 'stalemate' has a price, are you prepared to pay it?

↑ Lesson: Like all relationships, there will be relationship problems in your team. Commit to being part of the solution, recognise that being proactive, sincere, honest and open is the best way forward.

# Real commitment is needed for great relationships...

Every relationship has challenges and on any team there will be many but, as the saying goes "What doesn't kill you, makes you stronger." When a relationship isn't working, it's often the level of commitment that you have to it that will determine if it will survive, strengthen or break down. That level of commitment isn't easy, sometimes we pretend and think it will get better in time, it usually gets worse.

Sometimes, it might be hard, emotional, confronting, awkward even ugly but confronting the issues is the way forward. We have all had instances with parents, children, partners, husbands, wives, sisters, brothers etc, where because we really value the relationship we 'start again' with a real conversation. It's the same with your team, it's not always easy but the seeds of new growth in a relationship are planted by real conversations.

{ What doesn't kill you makes you stronger }

How committed are you to making the relationships with your team work?

"Real conversations are the ultimate commitment to a relationship. Real conversations are the **building blocks** of relationships. Real conversations are often the ones that you are most afraid to have."

**From the book 'Fish for life'**

# Proactive problem solving

We are in the people business and where you get people, you get problems. How do you handle problems on your team? When there is a problem, how do you usually react to it? Do you ignore it and hope it fixes itself? Do you sulk, scream, blame, deny, quit, bully? Or do you resort to verbal abuse, prescription drugs, alcohol, violence, substance abuse, attack verbally, ignore?

In a way they are all a form of communication but all with a negative outcome. None of these choices will solve the problem, it will either change the problem or it will just fester and get worse.

First thing is to recognise that problems are okay, they are just a normal part of everyday life but the key is to go about reacting to problems in a way that is most likely to produce a positive outcome.

{ Look upon problems as a chance to prove yourself }

### Focus on solving problems rather than having them
Look upon problems as a chance to prove yourself, imagine if you were seen as the 'go to' person for problem solving in your salon. What would that look like? What would the skills and personality of that person be? Calm, rational, patient, unflappable, in control, assertive ...sounds like a leader to me.

### Be accountable
Take the problem as yours to own and solve, do not just 'pass the buck' to someone else to sort out.

If it's conflict, be proactive and resolve it A.S.A.P.
In the hair and beauty industry because we have our clients in front of us, it is not always possible to resolve conflict with other team members immediately but the general rule of thumb is to be proactive. Take the initiative and make the effort to sit down with your team mates and sort out any problems at the earliest possible convenience.

### Don't attack the person
If the objective is to resolve the problem or reduce the chances of it happening again then be mindful to focus on the underlying reason it happened and not the person.

If a problem arises first look at the system for a solution.
In a business many things that cause problems are repetitive in nature, Seek to solve the problem but also look to how you can develop a system to prevent it happening again.

Avoid drama and generalisations

# Some people don't want solutions; they want "Soap Opera"

Now I know that in the hair and beauty industry because we are all such meek and mild personalities there is never any drama or sweeping generalisations in salons...is there?

But, just in case you ever come across that type of situation when there is a problem, take a deep breath, try not to make any sweeping generalisations where you use terms like…

- This is ALWAYS happening... or
- There is NEVER any... or
- EVERYTIME I go to get …

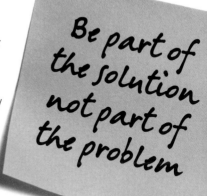

Be part of the solution not part of the problem

Sweeping generalisations like that are rarely accurate and only serve to make the problem worse.

Drama and the dramatic people that cause it is not always a bad thing. The hair and beauty industry is full of some very colourful and dramatic personalities and that sense of drama also brings life, vitality and passion to the business.

The flip side of all that drama is that the same people are often passionate, creative, fun, entertaining ...all the elements of a good salon. As the manager it's your role to manage those situations and people to bring about a positive outcome.

↑ Lesson: Learn to look at problems as opportuities and don't overreact. Challenges in business are just a normal part of everyday life, the key to success is to react in a calm, controlled manner as that is most likely to produce a positive outcome.

# Dealing with conflict

*"One of us is wrong...and it's not me! That's the sentiment that lies behind all conflict. If it didn't, it wouldn't be a conflict, would it?"*
(Quote from Seth Godin)

I don't know many people who wake up in the morning and can't wait to get to work so they can have some 'conflict'! Most of us hate being in personal or work situations where there is conflict.

The word 'conflict' itself describes why conflict is happening, it is because two or more people have conflicting, or different needs or views. Let me give some examples of the most common causes and possible solutions of how to handle conflict on your team:

## 1. Conflicting pressures
More often that not the client in a salon is seen by more than one person and we often have to depend on each other to get the work done. However, conflicts of need do arise. For example… what happens if you are a stylist and you need the only assistant in the salon to rinse off colour at the same moment that your team mate has an identical request with the same degree of urgency? It's inevitable that this type of thing is going to happen; it's easy to have a tantrum, pull rank or demand that more assistants are employed but that's not the real solution to the problem. There is no magic solution to every conflict of need but where possible try and plan ahead, anticipate each other's needs and reschedule other tasks and deadlines where possible.

Every issue demands clear communication. How can you help each other out? Is there a compromise? What can we juggle? Above all, be professional learn to juggle and compromise.

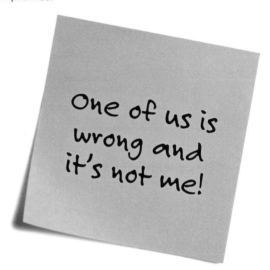

## 2. Conflicting personal values

Imagine that as the boss, you have organised an essential training session for everyone, when the time comes you are more than a little surprised to see that the very person who needs it the most has declared that they are unable to attend as it falls on a day that his/her faith observe as a religious holiday. What should come first the team or her faith?

Regardless of your beliefs, you have to recognise that at times there will be conflicting personal values in team members that conflict with the team values. There could be values like religion, children, family, health and partners and it's not up to me or anybody else to say what order of importance you should put them in. Our team is really important to us but we also need to respect and support the fact that we have different personal values. It's what makes us who we are.

{ Respect the fact that we have different personal values }

Obviously if this is a constant source of angst to the team and it happens with the same person at every training session then you might have identified a different kind of problem.

## 6. Conflicting roles

Whose job is it? Whose job is it to sweep up, shampoo, clean the staff room?

In every team there should be very clear roles, goals and responsibilities with individual job description, so that every one knows who is responsible for what. However this is a team you are on. Can you imagine if a footballer said "It's not my fault they scored a goal, it's not my job to stop it"

Everyone on your team has a job to do but the ultimate outcome is to make the client happy, so there will be times where everyone is required (without being asked) to see what the team, the business and the clients needs. If that means stepping out of your 'role' to clean the bathroom, shampoo a client, sweep up after someone, then regardless of your age, position, title, seniority get over yourself and do it …and do it with pride.

↑ **Lesson: Conflict is an inevitable part of being on a team and conflict can actually be very useful because it can encourage the conflicting parties to deal with it by communicating and as a result everyone benefits.**

"What is **tolerance?** It is the consequence of humanity. We are all formed of frailty and error; let us pardon reciprocally each other's folly – that is the first law of nature."

**Voltaire (François-Marie Arouet)**
**French writer**

# The need for tolerance

Not unique to the hair and beauty industry but everywhere in todays workplaces you will find that they are often filled with people from different backgrounds, ages, races, sexual orientation, viewpoints, and religions. To work well together, as a team, it's essential that everyone embrace and respect these differences. I find that those that are intolerant are usually acting out of fear and ignorance. No matter how different someone else may seem, the reality is we have far more in common than sets us apart.

Tolerance means keeping an open mind when interacting with others who are different from you and treating everyone with respect, even when you don't share their opinions or values. These differences can include race, ethnicity, religion, gender, sexual orientation, philosophy, values, physical abilities, and age. There might also be differences in viewpoints, family obligations, background, dress, work practices, political beliefs, attitude, education, and class.

{ Being tolerant means accepting others' behaviour }

When we work in an environment of tolerance on our team, not only does it encourage open honest communication, trust and respect but it also promotes creative thinking and innovation, improves team work and cooperation and encourages good working relationships. Tolerance also improves loyalty, and productivity – both of which are very important in the salon. Put simply, when you demonstrate understanding, empathy and respect to someone different from you, you're practicing tolerance.

Although being tolerant means accepting others' behaviour or viewpoints, it's not the same as indifference, indulgence or apathy. It doesn't mean accepting or justifying behaviour that is morally or ethically wrong or that is harmful to someone else. If you feel that the other people on the team are behaving badly or are doing something ethically or morally wrong, then you should know that it's okay to challenge that behaviour.

It's important to learn where to draw the line with tolerance. If someone is being hurt, or a person's words or actions are harming your mission, your team members or your salon, everyone on the team should know that it's acceptable to step in.

↑ Lesson: On a team it is essential that you embrace and respect differences and recognise that these differences help to make your team and the world we live in such a rich, diverse, and exciting place. Win:Win

"Your reputation and integrity are everything. Follow through on what you say you're going to do. Your **credibility** can only be built over time, and it is built from the history of your words and actions."

**Maria Razumich-Zec**

# Sorry about that Team, I stuffed up!

Will you? Damn right you will, everybody makes mistakes. When you do, what are you going to do about it? You are part of a team and when you 'stuff up' not only do you let yourself down but you let the team down as well. Your actions or lack of actions have an effect.

No one is perfect. We all do stuff, say stuff, forget stuff and generally have bad days. When we do, the best thing to do is apologise, clean it up, learn from it and move on. Sometimes that means that people have lost trust in us and as a result we have to earn that trust back, you build trust with integrity (doing what you say) and by the examples you demonstrate and set. If it's someone else on the team who has 'stuffed up' give them the same opportunity to set things right that you would expect them to give you.

> { No one is perfect, we all have bad days }

↑ Lesson: We all make mistakes. When you do 'admit it, learn from it, and move on'.

Make mistakes, learn from them and move on

# Meetings are a chance to really connect

Team meetings are an essential component of being on any team.

In the hair and beauty business because we have our clients in the same space as us, we often don't get the opportunities to communicate openly as a team. So having regular team meetings are essential to take the time to really connect as a team.

{ Contribute and communicate }

Often teams hate meetings. Why and how do we correct that? First of all understand what goes wrong, why do some people hate meetings?

The worst things about meetings are the same no matter where you go.
• Don't start on time, finish on time or stay on track
• Badly organised and lacking an agenda
• The same people do all the talking
• Too long and repetitive
• No one leading the meeting
• Everyone talking at once
• People coming late and leaving early
• No clear decisions, next steps or actionable items.

Meetings can and should be a positive experience. They are a great opportunity to connect, celebrate, encourage, inform and inspire. If you are organising or running the meeting, look at the list above. What can you do to avoid repeating the same mistakes?
• Plan ahead and be well prepared
• Start on time, finish on time
• Have an agenda
• Let people have their say but keep on track and make clear actionable decisions
• Keep the minutes and review progress at the next meeting
• Be in control.

How can you make the most of the meeting as an attendee?
• Be a grown up
• Be on time, (that means at least 5 minutes early)
• Participate actively and ask intelligent questions
• Follow through on delegated tasks
• Be positive, focus on solutions not problems.

Inspired by Sam Parker at givemore.com

↑ Lesson: Meetings and the chance for group discussion, is an essential part of being on a successful team. Everyone on the team has the responsibility to contribute and communicate in an open, honest and constructive manner.

# Feedback ...don't assume it's negative

Feedback is letting people know how they are performing. Don't make the mistake I did by assuming that feedback is always about telling people what they are doing wrong. My management mantra became "catch people doing something right ...and tell them". Then, when you do have to offer constructive feedback about something you are unhappy about it will be much better received and more likely acted upon.

People need to know how they are performing, they may not always want to know, or like, what they hear but they need to know. Likewise, you need to know their progress, how they are feeling and any challenges they may be experiencing. One of the most effective ways of developing your team is ensuring you give and get regular feedback.

Most managers are nervous about giving feedback, especially if it has to be negative. However, if you are someone who is always giving and receiving feedback everyone will come to expect it and everyone will benefit from improved performance.

**Giving effective feedback**

**Step 1: Feedback should be a positive experience for everyone**
Remember, that as a manager the reason you are giving feedback is to reinforce or improve the situation or performance of an individual. So the attitude with which you give feedback will have a huge influence on the end result. People respond better if your approach is positive and focused on improvement. If you are negative, sarcastic or condescending then you won't achieve the outcome you seek.

However, that isn't to say that there isn't a time to be angry or negative, there is and if it is appropriate show it but don't make that your standard approach. If it is, all you will achieve is individuals who are demotivated, disillusioned and fearful of doing anything lest they incur your rage.

Even when you do have to give negative feedback mix it up with the positive. I always try to work to the following formula:
Start by telling them what they are doing well
Then tell them what they are not doing well and need to do better
Finish on positive reinforcement of something that they do well.

If there is a particular 'negative issue' that really needs addressing, be careful not to overdo the positive. You need to make sure that there is no doubt in their mind concerning the nature of the issue and what action is required for them to address it.

I believe that most people want to do well, they want to please you but, I also believe most people are highly sensitive to being put down. The wrong approach will get their defences up and they will go straight into justification or denial mode. The only thing they will take away from the conversation will be the negative.

{ Make feedback constructive }

Making feedback constructive is a balancing act that often needs minute adjustments depending on who you are talking to, what the issue is, whether it has been previously addressed and what response you have had.

### Step 2: Timing is everything
Sometimes it is not appropriate to give someone immediate feedback. As a rule though the closer the feedback is to the event, the better. By keeping it timely the facts aren't distorted by the passing of time. The exception to this is, if people have become emotionally charged. If that is the case it is best to allow a little time to let everyone cool off, then it is less likely to result in someone saying or doing something that is later regretted.

### Step 3: Don't store it up
Giving constructive feedback is not about storing up all this 'stuff' to unleash on some poor unsuspecting soul. You don't want to attack and demoralise anyone, so don't store it up, deal with it when and as things happen.

### Step 4: Think it through and stick to the facts
It's easy to be spontaneous and casual when giving people positive feedback. However, when you are dealing with an issue that involves letting someone know that something is unsatisfactory and needs to change you need to be more prepared. Think through what you will say in advance, this will keep you focused on the issue at hand and not let you get sidetracked. Stick to the facts and don't make sweeping generalisations.

### Step 5: Praise in public, criticise in private
Use every opportunity to reinforce positive behaviour or results in front of clients or colleagues. The opposite applies if you are criticising someone's performance or behaviour, it should always be done in private and out of earshot of others.

### Step 6: If nothing changes ...nothing changes

Set clear next steps and expectations because "If nothing changes ...nothing changes."

There is no point in having a little pow-wow if nothing changes. Your job as the manager is to provide clear direction on addressing the situation. It is not about giving someone all the answers, as you need them to take ownership of solve the problem. I would ask them "What can I do to help you?" The crux of the message should be that you are there to help them grow and develop and that you will do whatever you can to help but that you can't do it for them. Define and agree on the next steps using the S.M.A.R.T acronym to set goals to ensure that they have the best chance of success.

Remember, S.M.A.R.T. stands for goals that are Specific, Measurable, Achievable, Results orientated and Time bound. It is important that they understand and agree on the goals, as they need to own the solution and are much more likely to follow through and implement if they do.

### Step 7: Follow up

When the purpose of feedback is to improve performance, it is essential that there is follow-up to ensure that change is being followed through and that there is improved performance as a result.

### Step 8: Tick all the boxes

The last step in the process is to document your conversations and keep a record of what has been agreed, what is working and what needs to be modified.

**Be the 'King of feedback'**

Feedback isn't a formal appraisal or target meeting. The key is giving constant feedback, that you notice everything both good and not so good and comment all the time. That way, problems never get out of hand and there are no surprises. Strive to give two bits of positive feedback for every bit of constructive criticism. Be the King (or Queen) of feed back!

## Remember, catch people doing something right ...and tell them.

Lesson: People need to know how they are performing. They may not always want to know, or like, what they hear but they need to know. If you are someone who is always giving and receiving feedback everyone will come to expect it and everyone will benefit from the improved performance.

# What you see is what you get...

Teams don't only work together in the physical sense. They also have a collective conscience; a universal way of thinking about issues, in both the positive and negative, the optimistic or pessimistic. Sometimes as a team in the pursuit of excellence, we focus too much on what isn't working, what we don't like or where we are going wrong. While it is important to always be looking for ways we can improve, if you only focus on what's wrong ...it's more than a bit demoralising. Take time to remind yourself and everyone else on the team what you are doing well because there undoubtedly will be many things that you do well.

In a very practical sense I am reminded of a time when our salon meetings would become nothing more than a series of complaints. I would stop them and say "Okay I want everyone in the room to say one good thing about working here, I don't care what it is, but I want one thing from everyone."  We would go around the room and everyone would have to say one good thing, it might be as small as "I really like the music we are playing in the salon" or "I just want to say how great it is to have Brian on the team, he is such a brilliant colourist" ...it didn't matter what they said but after we had gone around the room the energy level had changed completely. Even when things are tough, you must focus on what you can do and what you can control because what you focus on and think about is what you will experience.

{ Celebrate what you do well }

You must learn to focus on the solutions, not the problems. You must focus on the actions you can take today even if they are small ones and everytime you do something, you learn from it and find a way to do it better next time. Your mind is like a search engine, if you put in the word 'problem' then everything to do with problem comes up. If you put in the word 'solution' then that is what you will see, so choose to focus on where you want to go. Choose to focus on the solutions not the problems

What are you programming yourself for?

↑ Lesson: It is important to look at what is not working in your team and how to make it better but, don't forget to look for and remind yourself what is RIGHT and celebrate what you do well too.

# "7 times down, 8 times up"

**Japanese proverb**

# Checklist Chapter 5:
# Communication

- You cannot not communicate. So take responsibility to make all your communication positive and effective.

- A team is a series of relationships. As the manager you must build positive empowering relationships with everyone on the team.

- Great relationships require a real commitment. Be proactive in solving relationship problems. Be part of the solution not part of the problem.

- Real conversations are the ultimate commitment to a relationship, they won't always be easy but they are the key to moving forward.

- Team success has to be based on relationships that are win:win.

- Problems don't solve themselves. Be proactive and deal with them calmly and professionally. Always look for opportunities to address the problem, with solutions to avoid it happening again.

- You are not always going to agree with everyone on your team and that can create conflict. Deal with conflict professionally in the short term and look for longer term solutions to avoid the same issues being repeated.

- When you demonstrate understanding, empathy and respect to someone different from you, you're practicing tolerance.

- When you make mistakes, apologise, learn from it and move on.

- Team meetings are an essential time to communicate with the team, as the manager, you need to structure and control meetings to get the best use of everyone's time.

- Treat others how you want to be treated. Listen, don't be defensive and look for opportunities to reinforce all positive behaviour.

- It is easy for the team to always be looking at what isn't working, as the leader, take time to remind the team to also focus on what works!

# 6

## MAINTAINING YOUR TEAM

"The ultimate measure of a team is not where they stand in moments of comfort and convenience but where they stand at times of **challenge** and **controversy.**"

# The life cycle of the team...

A team is made up of people and people come and go, people have good days and bad days, people have lives outside the team that have an effect on what happens inside the team, people are emotional and sometimes dramatic but it's that emotion and drama that brings life and energy to the team. Teams aren't always on a high or a low, teams are like the seasons and with every season comes new opportunities, new challenges and new life. The team is evolving and in a perpetual state of change.

Sometimes that means people leaving and the morale and energy of the team might appear to leave with them and for those left the team morale can be at a low point. Questions are asked, both by and of, those remaining. Those questions give a renewed focus, purpose and commitment to the vision for the future.

{ Building a team is a constant and never ending journey }

When people leave the team it can be a good thing for everyone as often it gives others the opportunity to shine and grow into a new position, to 'spread their wings' and take on new and bigger responsibilities. As the manager, one of your jobs is to guide the team and the individuals in it through the various stages of growth and change. If you're not the manager but a member of the team, then your job is to evolve and grow, by contributing in a positive way by embracing change in the ongoing development of the team. Most of all, building a great team is not something 'you do and it's done, it's a constant and never ending journey. Everyone on the team is part of the solution, or part of the problem in the constant evolvement or reinvention of the team.

↑ Lesson: The very nature of teams is that they are about reinvention. No matter how successful the team is, you can't always stay on top. Often your real success can be found in how well you can constantly come back, hopefully bigger and better.

# Team retention

Team retention is like client retention, you grow the business by keeping the clients, not necessarily forever but if the average client stays with you for two years and you manage to increase that from two years to three years then you have grown the business. Team retention is the same, if your average team member stays with you for two years and you increase it to three years you have grown the business.

The key to growing your business is keeping your clients, and keeping your team because when a team member leaves, regardless as to whether they have 'opened up' next door or gone to the other side of the world, the end result is that you will lose clients. It's just a matter of how many.

There will always be some people on your team who need to, and want to move on and that's not a bad thing. However, there will be others that value the security, stability and camaraderie that exists within the team and they will want to stay and grow with you. As the manager, this entire book is about developing a great team, a team that people want to commit to and be a part of. Assuming you want people to stay, what are some of the key things that you need to make sure you do?

Firstly, I think it's important that you acknowledge that one fundamental truth is: 'although you are part of the team, you are different to the rest of the team'. You are the leader, the owner and or manager of the business, you probably have different motivations to your team members.

So recognise that you are not them and the things that motivate you, may not be what motivates them.

The mere fact that you are probably the one who opened the business ensures that you probably differ from the team on how you feel about values and emotions like 'risk, change and security'. What motivates them is different to what motivates you. If you want to retain people on your team, there are a few things that you need to consider. Ask yourself if they would be 'a fit' with the culture of your business.

- Have varied price levels, so that based on productivity your team has the opportunity to move up the scale and earn more without having to leave and go elsewhere.

- Create an ongoing personal development and training program for everyone on the team.

- Stay connected. Have regular six monthly appraisals with everyone on your team so that you keep in touch with the needs and aspirations of those on your team.

- Evolve the business and get your teams 'input and ideas' on how to do so.

- Understand what motivates the individuals on your team and look at ways to fulfil those needs.

- Have an ever-changing incentive and reward program.

- Acknowledge and reward productivity at an annual awards ceremony.

- Pay people well for their productivity but not at the expense of the business profit or the owner's income.

- Create a career path with opportunities for learning, financial and personal growth and promotion.

- Look for ways to expand and grow the business, this may mean expansion through opening more salons, partnerships, franchising, profit sharing etc. Accept that if you don't that some people will leave to pursue other growth opportunities.

- Take time to get to know your people at a deeper level; their life outside of work, their families and loved ones, the challenges and successes they face in life.

- Be there for them in times of crisis.

↑ Lesson: The key to growth is keeping high quality, motivated and productive people.

# How well do you address 'the six essential human needs'?

Anthony Robbins, the most successful motivational speaker and coach in the world today, defined 'the six essential human needs' and they are a great tool to understand what motivates people. Having a team of people that feel really committed and loyal to the business, is a question of understanding and fulfilling their six essential needs as human beings, not directly related to hairdressing, but as people.

{ What could you do that you aren't currently doing? }

**The six essential needs we all have are:**
**1. Certainty, 2. Uncertainty, 3. Significance,**
**4. Connection, 5. Growth , 6. Contribution**

How well do you address these six points?

## 1. Certainty
We all need to have a sense of order, control and security in our lives. As a manager, what do you do to make your team feel a sense of certainty and security in their jobs?
If your team don't feel a level of certainty, control and security, what chance is there of getting their full commitment and loyalty? How can you make your team feel a greater sense of certainty in their jobs?

## 2. Uncertainty
We need challenge and variety in the job we perform, we need an element of surprise, newness, stimulation? Is there an element of adventure and freedom for your team or is it mundane and boring? What systems have you put in place to ensure that all team members have variety in their daily tasks? That they are not constantly just doing dull, boring, mundane and repetitive jobs? What else could you do to get variety, mental and emotional stimulation and an element of the unknown into their daily routine?

## 3. Significance
We all need to feel important, needed and have a good sense of self worth. How significant do your team members feel? Regardless of their age or position, do they feel that they matter? Do they feel that what they do is important, that they are relied on and trusted to deliver an important component of the end-result? What processes do you have in place to ensure that your team feels needed and appreciated? What else could you do?

## 4. Connection

We have the need to communicate with, to belong to, and feel valued and appreciated by those around us. What level of connection do your team members feel to you, with each other? What processes do you have in place to encourage a greater level of engagement, communication, approval and connection with yourself and the rest of the team?

## 5. Growth

We each have the need for personal development, to grow, to become more, to evolve, to learn and to create meaning and purpose in our lives. What opportunities do you create for your team members to learn and grow?

What personal development opportunities do you create for your team to fulfil their potential not just in their jobs but as people? What else could you do?

## 6. Contribution

Contribution is about sharing what we have with others… giving back, serving others. How can you create opportunities for your team to feel that they are contributing?

People need to feel that they are part of something bigger and that they are contributing to the business and each others success, as well as the community they live and work in?

Is their contribution acknowledged? How can you develop opportunities to share what you have with others?

All of us are motivated and influenced by a combination of each of these six needs. They influence our thoughts, decisions and actions and make us the people that we are. The challenge we have as managers is how we accommodate and satisfy those needs into the fabric of a diverse range of individuals on our team. Look at what you currently do to motivate and satisfy the emotional needs of your people and give yourself an honest appraisal of your shortcomings and opportunities for improvement. As the manager, put together a list of action points and identify your top three to focus on.

With your team, look at the list of the six fundamental human needs and look for any areas that you could collectively improve.

↑ Lesson: We often look to short term solutions to motivate our people and while short term incentives, rewards and on-going acknowledgement is essential, we must not forget to examine the fundamental needs we have as human beings. Establish a business culture that will satisfy the deeper needs of the team.

# Make change positive!

Nothing stays the same and your team is no exception. The people on your team will come and go, sometimes you will be glad when people leave and sometimes you won't. Teams change and as a salon owner, the first time you have people leave it's upsetting. Get over it. What you have to do is make change positive. We have to embrace change and make it work for us. With every change there is an upside, granted that at first it may not always be evident but as you let go of one thing it makes way for something or someone else to fill the void.

When change is unexpected, for example if someone leaves unexpectedly, it will often throw you off balance. Take that as a positive, it's so easy to get comfortable with the status quo. When the carpet is pulled out from under your world it makes you reassess things. Toughen up and bounce back with that little bit more experience, so at very least you are better prepared next time. If you are the one instigating change, what is it that you want and how bad do you want it?

{ Nothing stays the same and your team is no exception }

If you want something to change in your life you have to do something differently. How much you really want change will be reflected by what you are prepared to do. The key words in that sentence are 'YOU' and 'DO'! "If you keep doing what you have always done, you will keep getting what you have always got". (If you're lucky.) It's easy to criticise and blame everyone else. It's harder to do something about it. Your life will change in direct proportion to how badly you want it to change and what YOU are prepared to DO about it!

If you really want to change something with your team, (or life in general) you'll find a way. If you don't, you'll find an excuse.

People on the team will come and go, our own lives are always in a state of change, the rules of the game are constantly changing, the economy is constantly changing, the world we live in is constantly changing, the relationships we have are constantly changing ... It's a game, and it's called 'change or perish'. I choose change.

↑ Lesson: Change is not something you have a choice about. Change is constant. What you do have choice about is how you perceive and react to change. Always look for the upside.

# Win:Win

Your destiny and that of your team is entwined. You cannot have and maintain successful employers without successful employees. Our business and financial destinies are linked with our teams individual financial success. The only way the business wins is if the individual wins and vice versa.

In business we often end up with an 'us and them' culture where it is always about 'winning' at the other party's expense. Businesses and individuals that operate like that are short lived; the only way to really grow is to grow and reward your team within the business. If they are achieving their own personal goals balanced with the salon owners goals, then success will be ongoing therefore creating a state of win:win for everyone.

If you get the balance wrong and you have a situation where senior team members are better rewarded financially than the owner, success isn't sustainable and will only breed contempt and bitterness. Conversely if the owner is making all the money and trying to keep productive people on a minimal wage it will create unrest. Team members will leave to either decide to go elsewhere or start their own business. Both of these scenarios are common place.

I am always amazed at how many salon owners pay some of their team members more than themselves and justify it by saying, if they didn't the staff would leave. "Who's working for whom?" Either scenario has no future, it's just a matter of how long they last.

↑ Lesson: It's about people building people, not 'us and them'.

Embrace change and make it work for you?

"

"The only way the business wins is if the individual wins and vice versa."

**WIN:WIN**

# As the business has goals, so should the individual...

As the business has goals, so should the individual, as it is only through individual achievement that the business achieves its goals. So what are the individuals' goals? What is the vision they have for themselves? One of the many roles of the leader is getting the individuals on the team focused on their future and getting them to realise that hairdressing is the vehicle by which they can achieve their personal, financial and life goals. This is not only a worthy role for the leader but will also contribute to the business achieving the established vision in harmony with the goals of the team member, team and the business.

Many young hairdressers think about as far ahead as their next haircut (I know, because that is exactly what I did) but, eventually a point in time arrives, call it ambition, call it enthusiasm or just call it 'getting older', regardless of what you call it, it culminates in wanting to have, to get, to do and become 'more' and it starts by having the vision of what 'more' means.

{ to have, to get, to do 'more' }

What is the vision that team members have for themselves? Is their vision in alignment with the rest of the team and the goals of the business? What might those goals and objectives look like for an individual on the team? They might be:

- To establish their own clientele by a certain date
- To win the salon retail competition for the year
- To produce their first photographic collection
- To enter the hairdressing awards this year
- To have the highest amount of referral clients in the salon for the year
- To have the highest colour percentage in the salon for the month
- To be the highest revenue producer in the salon for the year
- To be promoted to senior stylist by a certain date
- To increase their personal income by 25% this year.

Is it in alignment with the salon goals? If you don't have ambition and clear goals? What chance is there of it happening?

↑ Lesson: As the business has goals, so should the individual, as it is only through individual achievement that the business achieves its goals.

# Getting people to be at their best...

Possibly the biggest challenge we face as managers is motivating our people to be at their best. What are the tools we have at our disposal? Many people are motivated by money and money is very important to all of us. However money alone is not enough. On a day-to-day basis, in any business, numerous opportunities present themselves to motivate the team (or individuals within it) through offering incentives for improved performance. While these incentives serve a definite purpose and are an important tool in creating a fun competitive element to the day, they are not the key to long term motivation and real commitment. Real motivation comes from your people buying into something bigger.

## How do you motivate your team to get things done?

If your technique involves yelling louder, pushing harder and relentlessly badgering your team to produce better results, good luck... It won't work (or if it does, it won't last). People can be pushed to get things done but when the pushing stops, so do the results. If the team responds to your habit of yelling for results, when the yelling stops, so do the results.

{ The best motivator, in my experience, is praise. }

If your work environment is built on verbal chastisement to get results, what is the likelihood that a place like that would genuinely inspire people and build a positive happy and loyal culture?

Promoting a culture of healthy competition can be a strategy for achieving results. So motivate people by sharing and comparing results. Post the results of client retention, client counts or service figures on the staffroom notice board at the end of each week and you will soon see nobody wants to be at the bottom. Many people will respond to that type of competition and in the short term at least this may work. The problem is that like all competitions you can only have one real winner which means most of the team members are...losers. For some people losing will motivate them to try harder next time but others give up and don't try at all creating a negative impact on the rest of the team. The problem is that in a business you don't want only one winner, you want the whole team and the business overall to be the winner. The other downside of competitions is that you are trying to develop a team of people that help and support each other so it's hard to create that team dynamic when at the same time you are competing against each other.

# What is the key to long term results?

When your people learn to embrace achievement they get addicted to it. If you can coach and encourage, develop and nurture them by celebrating their achievements, you will create lasting results. Results that can never be achieved through rivalry and yelling. The best motivator in my experience is praise. Acknowledgement is proof that a team member's performance has been noticed and that they did a good job. It's acknowledgement that you noticed they were trying and improving and it only took a few seconds. Sometimes, it was just a smile or a wink... but you noticed and that praise is a huge motivator. Left to their own devices, most people are unable to manage and motivate themselves to fulfil their potential. Providing guidance and encouragement, for even the most reluctant team member, will produce amazing results.

A truly successful business is built through mutual team support and the understanding that the team is responsible for their own goals and that they are part of something bigger. When you can do this, you give people and the business an amazing platform to grow.

↑ Lesson: Motivation takes many forms and different people respond to different things. The best motivator, in my experience, is praise. Acknowledgement is proof that a team member's performance has been noticed and that they did a good job.

Positive behaviour that gets reinforced gets repeated

# Practical ways to reward, give recognition and acknowledgment...

To really connect and engage with your team at a deeper level requires taking ongoing communication to the next level. You have to do what everyone else isn't doing. You have to go the extra mile.

Here's a few suggestions for managers, some of them might cost a little but many of them are free and will have an impact on your teams level of motivation.

**Write personal thank you notes on pay slips:**
It doesn't have to be a lot but a few simple words such as "Thanks for all your input this week" or "I really appreciated your help with training this week" or "It was excellent the way you handled that complaint yesterday" goes a long way.

{ Let your team know that you notice and appreciate them }

Taking the time to notice and acknowledge the small things makes all the difference. The key point is to use the opportunity to personally acknowledge them, to let your team know that you notice and appreciate them.

**Praise your team in front of their peers during weekly meetings:**
Give constructive criticism in private but praise in public. Use every opportunity to acknowledge individual achievement and progress in front of their peers. Give them a higher standard to live up to.

**Give cash incentives for ideas that improve the business:**
Awarding cash incentives for ideas that improve the business, not only encourages employees to think of how they can earn more money but also gets them to take more interest and pride in what they are doing.

**Celebrate anniversaries of service:**
No one remembers what day they started but if YOU do, it's a significant brownie point, so make sure you acknowledge the anniversary. Whether it's just a card to celebrate their anniversary of service or perhaps a small gift that changes for each year of service, celebrate each anniversary. It's as simple as making a note in your diary when someone starts.

**Recognise outstanding performers in an annual awards ceremony:**
Have an annual awards ceremony to acknowledge achievement. As well as the obvious awards for highest productivity, also look for opportunities to award improvement, great customer service, the most helpful team member or best dressed.

**Organise a financial consultant to meet with the team:**
Look for opportunities to educate and inspire your team outside of the skills normally associated with their job. For example: organise a financial consultant to meet with your team, to give them advice on getting out of debt, using credit cards effectively, or a savings plan for a mortgage.

**Organise company bowling, volleyball, golf day:**
Team building days outside of the normal training plan help people bond and get to know each others skills outside of the normal work environment.

**Host an employee of the month award:**
Look for opportunities to acknowledge your outstanding team members for achievement in any areas from service to productivity or appearance.

**Relevant incentives, i.e. driving lessons, gym pass:**
Make motivational incentives relevant – to those who you are trying to motivate. Where a weekend away or a massage might motivate a 30 year old an 18 year old is more likely to be motivated by driving lessons, a travel pass, concert tickets or an iTunes voucher.

**"Thanks for your help today":**
Never forget the value of appreciation. You can never do it too much, make it your commitment to thank everyone with a few kind words of acknowledgment every day.

↑ Lesson: Rewards, recognition and acknowledgement needn't always involve expense. You have to do what everyone else isn't doing, go the extra mile.

*What else can you do to give recognition and acknowledgement?*

"It is only by helping others to achieve their goals that you will achieve yours."

# Developing leadership in others...

Part of the growth of your business is dependent on your ability to develop leadership in others within your team, for two reasons. Firstly, if you don't, it's only a matter of time before the natural leaders in your team want to move on. Secondly, if you want to grow the business, you need to be endeavouring to make yourself redundant! By that I mean that you should be continually releasing your time in order to free yourself up to grow the business and not have the business consume your time with 'running the business'.

## People are like plants, if they stop growing they die.

I don't mean die in the literal sense, I mean that if they are not being challenged and given opportunities that stretch them and make them grow then inevitably they will become bored and look elsewhere for those opportunities.

{ Free yourself up to grow the business }

↑ **Lesson: Give potential leaders an understanding that they can have a bright future within the business and actively create and plan opportunities to offer that bright future.**

*Develop Leaders*

# Leadership problems

**Avoid unwilling leaders**
It is important to understand that not everyone wants the responsibility of leadership. Recognise that just because someone does a good job at one level doesn't mean they will do a good job at another. Unwilling leaders don't want responsibility, so think carefully about who your potential leaders are.

**The title doesn't equal the power**
Real leadership is earned not given, just because someone is given a title of Creative Director, Manager or Head Receptionist, it doesn't mean they have the respect, the power or the co-operation that leaders develop over time.

{ Real leadership is earned not given }

**Beware of unofficial leaders**
Unofficial leaders can be your greatest allies by offering back room support and loyalty where you need it most but, unfortunately they can also be an incredibly destructive force, undermining your every move through their lack of support or blatant staffroom sabotage of your plans and objectives.

Know who your unofficial leaders are, they probably don't have a title but in the staffroom or in the pub after work they hold an enormous amount of influence over the rest of the team not just by their words but by what they do or don't do. Your job is to turn them into a force for good and get them onside.

↑ **Lesson: Leadership is a double edged sword**

# Stay connected

Be present as the leader. It's so easy for you as the leader, owner and manager to get distracted by other projects which seem to be a priority; projects that pull you away from your most precious resource, your people. Your team need to feel connected with you. They need to know their leader is present and that you notice and care about their work, their ideas and their lives. It is so easy to get bogged down in your own world and as a result lose that connection with your team.

You spend a lot of time developing your company culture and your culture demands ongoing care and attention or it can quickly implode. Ignore your people and you are destroying your company from within. Staying connected means being available and knowing who to talk with to get an instant barometer on team morale. Staying connected means not just paying lip service to people but really understanding their issues.

If you can stay connected to your people they are far more likely to go the extra mile for you when you need it. You are more likely to have their loyalty, their trust and their commitment.

↑ Lesson: Be present as the leader, your team needs to feel connected with you.

In business your most precious resource is your people

# Drinkin' and druggin'

We live in a world where substance abuse is rife and there is no point in pretending otherwise. In some career paths it's the norm to spend evenings having a few drinks and in some career paths there is a casual acceptance about recreational drug use. While the few drinks are legal and the recreational drugs aren't, both can be equally damaging, not just to your business but to peoples lives. What you do in your personal life is up to you, we all make choices in life, we all sometimes make the wrong choices. I'm not Saint Antony and I'm not taking some moral high ground for the sake of it.

But, there has to be a couple of absolute hard and fast rules.

Firstly, if you are getting drunk and using illegal substances with your team you are doing untold damage to your credibility as a manager. Sure, one or two of them might think you are really cool but for the majority you have just lost all respect. Game over. Finito.

> { If anyone is selling or using drugs they must be sacked }

Secondly, when we talk about drug abuse, the rule of thumb is that if anyone is selling or using drugs within your business they must be sacked on the spot. It is a zero tolerance issue. Fire them there and then; it's not even open for discussion.

As the leader you have a real responsibility to the people on your team

# Now for the grey areas

As a manager you have a degree of responsibility to the health and welfare of the people you employ. In some industries, hairdressing, fashion and music for example, you often have very young and very impressionable teenagers in your employ. You have a real moral duty to offer them some guidance both through the examples you set, and the position you take on these issues.

As a salon owner or manager you are often in a position of trust and credibility that perhaps your team members don't have at home and you can make a real difference to the choices they make in life. Don't take that responsibility lightly. The reality is that many people will develop addiction issues and you are in a position of authority where, depending on the case, you can help a fellow human being get their life back together.

It is case dependent and there are many variables to consider but no one is perfect and if a member of your team has 'gone off the deep end' you quite simply have a chance to help them. That help, might take the form of time off, it might be financial, it might be organising the resources they need to get into rehab, it might be just being a friend and getting them to confront their issues and be able to talk about it with someone they respect.

Will you always be successful? No.

Will you often be let down and disappointed by them? Yes.

Might they steal from you, lie and cheat? Yes.

## Is it worth trying? Definitely.

Because when you save someone from a life of self destruction, it is probably one of the best things you can do.

Just know when to stop.

You can only do so much. You can't save people from themselves.

↑ Lesson: As a manager you have a moral responsibility for the health and welfare of the people you employ. You have a duty to offer them some guidance both through the example you set and the position you take on these issues. Set the right example.

# Know when it's time to cut them loose...

## Don't carry dead wood.

We live in an over-legislated society. It is what it is. It's the law and if you are in business, you have to adhere to the employment laws of wherever you do business. Depending on what country you are in most employees are very aware of their rights and who to go to when they feel their rights are being violated. Employment laws and unfair dismissal laws are predominantly in favour of the employee not the employer, so you have to have ticked every box, crossed every 't' and dotted every 'i', to ensure the law is on your side.

{ Ensure the law is on your side }

I'm not for one minute suggesting that you violate someone's rights but for the betterment of the business, the clients, the team and often the individual in question, there are times when it is in everyone's interest that you let someone go. Sack them, fire them, move them on, cut them loose... The only option open to you is to make sure that you use the law to your advantage and set up a business that conforms to all the legal requirements. Then when you do need to let someone go, you are being fair and reasonable. If you have followed the processes and documented everything along the way, you are in a better position to protect your business and you will probably, possibly, hopefully be alright.

When you look at professional athletes they live and die by their performance. If they don't measure up, they are cut from the team very quickly and they sit on the bench waiting for an opportunity to get back in, to prove their worth. The success and the needs of the team supersede those of the individual; you live and die by your performance.

In business, although perhaps it should be more like that, it has become anything but. I will often see situations where someone should have left or been moved on long ago but for a whole range of reasons they are still there. The result is that the whole business is hampered by someone who for a whole variety of reasons isn't a 'fit' anymore and is like a cancer in the business.

# You have three choices;

**You accept it**
**You change it**
**You end it.**

### If you accept it
You are accepting that someone isn't performing to the level required. Now, assuming you are being reasonable, you are saying to the rest of the team and clients "I have lowered my standards and expectations to this level of performance". Again, where is your pain threshold? What are you prepared to accept? What is negotiable and what is non-negotiable? You have to decide because the success of your business is at stake and this can drag on and on for years and destroy your business from within.

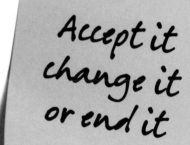

### If you decide to change it
You are sending out a message that says "this is not acceptable, and we are going to change it". Now, the rest of the team is clear on where the line is drawn and the individual concerned understands that they have to change or deal with the consequences. As the manager you offer every bit of support, training and encouragement to bring about a positive benchmarked change within an agreed time frame.

### Your final choice is, you end it
Now, no one is in any doubt about how serious you are about your vision, your standards and your levels of expectation. You act within your rights, you have established all the legal criteria to get you to this point and you end it. It might cost you money in redundancy, depending on the country you are in you may even be sued for unfair dismissal which is why you need to follow the letter of the law but, whatever happens you are still in control. You are still in charge and you have set the standards.

If you fail to manage and control your team they will control your income and your reputation.

## It's your move.

↑ Lesson: Never be afraid to cull underperformers.

# Have fun

Show me someone who's enjoying their job and I'll show you someone who's doing a good job. Teams experience a broad range of emotions but the underlying emotion should be 'fun'. Fun is a positive energy, the more energy you have the more passion you have and the more people want to be around you. You spend more of your time at work than you do at home so you better enjoy what you do and like sharing time with the people you do it with. Having fun at work is an attitude, a state of mind which not only benefits everyone on the team but clients too. Clients enjoy an atmosphere in which they enjoy themselves, it lightens their day and makes them feel good.

For those people who have fun at work, the work itself becomes a reward not just a way of earning.

{ The more energy you have the more passion you have }

## Fun is a choice. You decide to either enjoy your day…or not.

- Don't confuse fun with being unprofessional
- Happy people treat each other well
- Fun leads to creativity
- Time passes quickly
- Having a good time not only feels good, it is good for you
- Having fun is cyclical – the more fun you have …the more fun you have.

↑ Lesson: Fun is a positive energy, the more energy you have, the more passion you have and the more people want to be around you.

# Celebrate. Celebrate. Celebrate.

Often when you watch sport, any sport, you see a team that score or wins and immediately there is a spontaneous celebration, it might be jumping on each other, hugging, drenching each other with champagne, high five, back slapping… Then often immediately after the celebration the whole tempo of the game is raised to another level. The goal, or win and the celebration itself improves the level of energy and therefore performance and the team often goes on to score again soon after.

How can you celebrate your wins? When someone on your team has a 'win' how can you celebrate it, should you even celebrate it?

## Hell yeah! Is the unequivocal answer.

It's been proven again and again and again that positive behaviour that is reinforced is repeated. That principal applies whether you are talking about training your pet, your spouse, your children, your staff, your colleagues …or yourself. 'Positive behaviour that gets reinforced gets repeated'. Celebrating in any shape or form is reinforcing the behaviour as 'good', as a win, as success!

> Positive behaviour that gets reinforced gets repeated

### What is a win in a salon?
You can celebrate… a great haircut or colour, or an exceptionally productive day. You can celebrate a stylist achieving a 'first' such as their first haircut or colour unassisted, or the first time they have reached £100 or £1,000 or £2,000 in revenue, or maybe they just handled a really difficult situation extremely well. The point is, that all day long people are performing and people are getting results and good results should always be celebrated because 'positive behaviour that gets reinforced gets repeated' and the whole tempo of the game goes up another level.

### So what does that look like in your salon?
I'm not suggesting that you run around the salon high five'ing, or hugging each other every time someone has a 'win' but, I am suggesting that at the very least you acknowledge it. That may take the form of a wink, a thumb's up, a card, a post it, a group email, a Facebook post, a verbal "well done, great haircut!" Or, a scrawled message on the salon notice board… Do something that celebrates and acknowledges every and any occasion that deserves it, using whatever means and whatever platitudes you feel are appropriate to suit the occasion.

↑ Lesson: Look for ways to acknowledge and celebrate any results, actions or behaviours that you want to be part of your team culture.

# Thank you! Thank you! Thank you!

It doesn't take much, and it doesn't cost anything but simple common courtesies all day everyday, with everyone always, makes a huge difference to the dynamic of the team. It starts with a courteous morning welcome and smile, a "Good morning, how are you today?" and it's important that you really mean it, you need to make eye contact and take that split second to engage and connect with them as a person. You might be thinking "Well it's part of the job, so why do I need to say please and thank you all the time?" It's simple. It's good manners and your team feels good about the way you communicate. You don't really need any other reason.

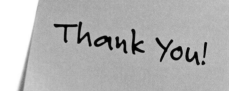

"Could you shampoo for me please?"
"Please could you stay back and help me tidy up?"
"I need you to do a consultation please?"

"Thanks for doing my shampoo."
"Thanks for tidying up."
"Thanks for doing that consultation."

## It's just good manners.

It doesn't always have to be verbal. I know of a salon where every team member has a small A4 size white board on the wall in the staff room and as well as writing reminders all the team regularly write little thank you notes to each other on them.

Lastly, when the day is finished how hard is it to say "Have a good evening and thanks for your help today it was really appreciated".

↑ Lesson: Common courtesies create a positive an energy. We should commit any small act of kindness we can to reinforce a culture of caring and sincerity.

# Never stop learning and growing…

Most people enjoy learning and growing at every stage of their life and for me that is what youth really is. However, for whatever the reason there are many people who somewhere along the line unfortunately stop learning and growing.

Commit to being a life long learner. Be open to new ideas and insights. Continually invest both time and money into your ongoing education. In reality the only asset you have is your mind, the most powerful tool you have under your own control. Recognise that time is your most precious asset and how you spend it is your choice. You can choose to watch TV or you could choose to read a book or master a skill. Alternatively you could learn about people, history, music, money, art, business, whatever interests you. You become what you study!

{ Be brave and take the next step and pursue your new dream }

One of the things I love about the hair and beauty business is that it is predominantly a young persons industry. We are surrounded by young people with new ideas, new music, new ways of thinking, new standards, new beauty aesthetics, new values. While you may not always agree or like 'the new', both what we do professionally and in life generally is all about change. So, it is essential that we continue to learn new ways of living in the world. If nothing else it keeps you young.

So be an explorer of life, be hungry for new ideas, be open and receptive to new ways of doing things and looking at the world, be curious and ambitious up until the final whistle.

↑ Lesson: "When you're green you grow, when you're ripe you rot."

# Know when it's time to go

Whether you are the owner or a member of the team there might come a day when it's time to go, when you no longer feel that you want to be part of the team that you are currently on. That's not always a bad day, maybe it's time, time for you to move on and follow another path.

If or when that day comes, be brave and take the next step and pursue your new dream

## Good luck.

# Maintaining the team

- The nature of teams is that they are continually evolving and you won't always be on top. As the manager one of your jobs is to guide the team and the individuals within it through the various stages of growth and change.

- The key to growth is keeping high quality, motivated and productive people. Look for opportunities for your team to grow and develop both creatively and financially within your business.

- To have a team of people that feel really committed and loyal to the business is more than just about money. You need to understand and fulfil their 'six essential needs' as human beings.

- Change is inevitable, so make it positive. Always look for the upside.

- Celebrate the successes of everyone on the team, look for practical low cost ways to reward and recognise good performance on the team.

- As the leader it is essential that you stay connected with your team, they need to feel you are there and that you understand their issues.

- When it comes to drink and drug abuse, as a manager you have a moral responsibility for the health and welfare of the people you employ. You have a duty to offer them some guidance both through the example you set, and the position you take on these issues. Set the right example.

- There is a time when some people are no longer contributing to the team in the way they need to. Never be afraid to cull underperformers.

- Work should be fun. Fun is a positive energy, the more energy you have, the more passion you have and the more people want to be around you.

- Common courtesies are not just polite they help create a positive energy in the team.

- What are some tangible ways that will create improved leadership in the team?

- Be a life long learner, never stop learning and growing.

- Building a team is a never ending process, this work is never finished.

- Know when it's time to go and move on to find your new passion.

"

"Building a great team is not about something you do and it's done ...it's a **constant** and never ending journey."

# Learning Resources of Antony Whitaker

## Increase your effectiveness
## Increase your income

ANTONY WHITAKER BUSINESS PROGRAMS
The keys to making a quantum leap in your life and career.

ANTONY WHITAKER
SPEAKER, TRAINER, SEMINAR LEADER, BUSINESS COACH

Antony Whitaker is one of the top professional speakers in the hairdressing world, addressing more than 250,000 people in excess of forty countries. Antony's keynote speeches, talks and seminars are described as "passionate, inspiring, emotive and real".

Contact us today for full information on booking Antony to present one of his seminars or to speak at your next meeting or conference.

Visit www.growmysalonbusiness.com
or email antony@growmysalonbusiness.com

"

"There is no one on the planet that delivers such an **honest and open** dialogue with hairdressers!"

**Peter Hedge**
**Oscar Oscar**
**Melbourne**

# Seminars

## Seminar 1: 'Super stylist'

**As a salon owner the key to business growth is growing each and every individual.** The emphasis with this seminar is on getting the team members motivated to take ownership of their productivity by giving them both the understanding and the skills to enable them to increase their clientele and the revenue they generate.

## Seminar 2: 'The Empowered Salon'

**The successful salons of today and tomorrow** are the ones that can harness the passion and commitment of their people to foster the values of constant improvement. Constant improvement as a way of life in building a better salon business can only be achieved by empowering your team to take ownership of their jobs, so they take a personal interest in improving the performance of the salon.

## Seminar 3: 'Management'

**Successful businesses start with strong foundations.** Holding most businesses back from reaching their full potential is a lack of clear objectives and a workable plan to turn those goals into reality. The 'Management' seminar is the beginning of a business and marketing action plan for your business.

## Seminar 4: 'Money'

**Is your business an asset or a liability?** You will not and cannot grow if you are not financially astute. If you want a successful business you have to be on top of the finances or it will destroy you. The harsh reality is that the majority of small businesses fail; the danger is that most business operators run the business out of their heads without the proper operating systems. 'Show me the Money' is about developing the financial operating systems you need to succeed.

## Seminar 5: 'Marketing'

**The key to successful marketing is reaching people** who already want to buy what you sell. The challenge is, who are they and how do you get to them? 'Marketing' is about tailoring solutions and systems to increase the amount of new clients coming through your door, turning them into regulars and keeping them as long as possible

# Seminar 6: 'Team building for teams'

**Your future success now**, more than ever, is determined by your ability to build, train and maintain a team. As the owner, your job is to grow people into a united team that represents your brand. The 'Team building for teams' seminar is a totally interactive day for owners/managers and their teams.

# Seminar 7: 'Team building for owners/managers'

**Turning the company vision of growth into reality** is dependent on inspiring and empowering a management team whose job is to recruit, train and grow people into a united team that represents your brand. The 'Team building for owners/managers' seminar is the beginning of creating the business management systems you need to succeed.

# Seminar 8: 'Retailing for professionals'

**For many salons retailing is the lost opportunity** to not only give clients 100% service and the benefit of their professional expertise but also to capitalise on the potential for significant extra revenue. You will finish the day inspired and motivated to capitalise on this huge missed opportunity.

For further information on the Antony Whitaker seminar program visit:

www.growmysalonbusiness.com

or email antony@antonywhitaker.com

# Testimonials

*"Great presenter, exceeded expectations, I learned soooo much. Thank you. I cannot think of a more efficient class."*
Char Panico-Muffitt, Chicago

*"Inspirational! A total game changer, I will be setting my sights higher with all aspects of my life, not just hairdressing"*
Beth Allison Spruicll, Bond Academy, New York

*"I loved this class! It was a great experience. Definitely a great class to take while starting out on my career."*
Aleshia Zimmerman, Indianapolis

*"Fantastic! You recognised everyone's different experience level, I never once thought, 'This doesn't apply to me'. Everyone can take something away, simple useful ideas that are easy to apply."*
Christin Stevens, Chicago

*"He reinforces everything I believe in and I am passionate about as a salon owner and brings it to you in a very energetic and fun way. This is something every new stylist should know before they begin their career."*
Linda Williams, Indianapolis

*"Very, very clear, easy to understand and implement. Our whole team has been exposed to an easy to understand and easy to implement program that has everyone on the same page."*
Corinne Kleinburger, Florida

*"Energetic, positive, kept my attention and made me realise that even after 27 years I still have so much to learn."*
Tim Belcher, Miami

*"Antony is truthful and honest about what's really important about the beauty industry, he teaches the steps to become different and special. He is changing the industry one hairdresser at a time."*
Jennifer Correale, New York

*"Antony you are an inspiration every time I hear you speak. You are great at what you do. Thanks"*
DJ Alexander, Ontario

*"Fantastic! Holy grail in idiot proof format"*
Aaron Giamattei, Berkshire

*"Great team-builder and hits all the important points to be successful!"*
Kevin Hawkins, New York

*"Excellent! My Brain hurts! Everything I learnt today will be beneficial for years to come."*
Annette Greene, Denver

*"Excellent presentations. Relevant and clear. It has made us refocus on aspects of our business that have become stale and inspired our team to look at the business through new eyes."*
Philip McCarthy, Wales

*"Antony is simply motivating. He relates well to all types of personalities/hairdressers. Very useful information that will expand myself and the business."*
Lorraine Buchanan, Brisbane

*"Amazing educator, straight to the point and doesn't sugar coat anything which is awesome. I have never gotten so much out of a seminar before!"*
Jo Lavers, Brisbane

*"Fantastic! A real innovator and educator. Very passionate about what he's saying."*
Jack Rendle, Portsmouth

*"If you just do one seminar this year, make it this one!"*
Leah Hunter , Sydney

*"Genius! If you are serious about your business and your profession you must attend. Great work, engaging and inspiring."*
Heath Lavingdale, London

*"A huge amount of enthusiasm for making sure we all get it. As a salon owner I cannot think of a better way to get the whole team on the same page"*
Matt Hudson, Annapolis

*"I can feel my income growing as I sit in this seminar. Antony is extremely motivating and his theories on how to grow your business are easy to understand and make perfect sense, I can't wait to get started"*
Michelle DeMatteis, Annapolis

# Contact

For more information, to contact Antony Whitaker or to subscribe
to the GROW free business building newsletters, seminars
bookings, read testimonials or visit the online shop see the authors
web site at www.growmysalonbusiness.com

Published by Antony Whitaker © Antony Whitaker
Edited by Rachel Gould
Designed by Karen Wilks www.karenwilks.co.uk
Printed by PUSH www.push-print.com